After the War

After the War

The Last Books of the Mahabharata

Translated by
WENDY DONIGER

OXFORD
UNIVERSITY PRESS

Oxford University Press is a department of the University of Oxford. It furthers the University's objective of excellence in research, scholarship, and education by publishing worldwide. Oxford is a registered trade mark of Oxford University Press in the UK and certain other countries.

Published in the United States of America by Oxford University Press
198 Madison Avenue, New York, NY 10016, United States of America.

© Oxford University Press 2022

All rights reserved. No part of this publication may be reproduced, stored in a retrieval system, or transmitted, in any form or by any means, without the prior permission in writing of Oxford University Press, or as expressly permitted by law, by license, or under terms agreed with the appropriate reproduction rights organization. Inquiries concerning reproduction outside the scope of the above should be sent to the Rights Department, Oxford University Press, at the address above.

You must not circulate this work in any other form
and you must impose this same condition on any acquirer.

CIP data is on file at the Library of Congress
ISBN 978-0-19-755339-8 (hbk)
ISBN 978-0-19-755340-4 (pbk)

DOI: 10.1093/oso/9780197553398.001.0001

1 3 5 7 9 8 6 4 2

Paperback printed by Lakeside Book Company, United States of America
Hardback printed by Bridgeport National Bindery, Inc., United States of America

Contents

Acknowledgments	ix
Introduction	1
Part I: The Text and the Story	1
The Older Generation: The Birth of Pandu, Dhritarashtra, and Vidura	5
The Birth of the Sons of Pandu and Kunti	9
The Marriage of Draupadi	10
Part II: The Last Books of the *Mahabharata*	13
Book Fifteen (Living in the Ashram) and Book Eleven (The Women)	14
Book Sixteen (The Battle of the Clubs), Gandhari's Curse, and Buddhist and Jain Variants	18
Book Seventeen (The Great Departure) and Yudhishthira's Dog	20
Book Eighteen (Climbing to Heaven) and the Transfer of *Karma*	24
Part III: The Meaning of the End of the Story	28
Death and Transfiguration	28
Theodicy and the Cause of Devastating War	31
Vengeful Pride as a Cause of War	36
Part IV: An Apology for My Translation	39
Criticizing the Critical Edition, and Leaving Key Words in Sanskrit	39
The Problem of Adjectives and Epithets	41
The Poet and His Formulas, or Parry and Lord to the Rescue	48

THE TRANSLATION

Book Fifteen, *Ashramavasika Parvan*, The Book of Living in the Ashram: Chapters 26–47	55
Preface to Book Fifteen	55

Part One: Living in the Ashram 56
  Chapter 26: Narada Arrives and Predicts Dhritarashtra's
    Arrival in Heaven 56
  Chapter 27: Narada Predicts Dhritarashtra's Worlds 58
  Chapter 28: The Pandavas Worry about Their Mother and
    Dhritarashtra 59
  Chapter 29: The Pandavas Set Out for the Forest 60
  Chapter 30: The Pandavas Enter the Forest with Their Army 62
  Chapter 31: The Pandavas Meet Kunti, Dhritarashtra, and
    Gandhari 64
  Chapter 32: Sanjaya, the Bard, Introduces the Pandavas to
    the Hermits 65
  Chapter 33: Vidura Enters the Body of Yudhishthira 67
  Chapter 34: Yudhishthira Distributes Gifts and Vyasa Arrives 70
  Chapter 35: Vyasa Explains Who Vidura Was and Offers to
    Perform a Miracle 72
Part Two: The Vision of the Sons 74
  Chapter 36: Narada Arrives and Dhritarashtra Grieves 74
  Chapter 37: Gandhari Tells Vyasa of the Women's Grief 76
  Chapter 38: Kunti Tells Vyasa How She Abandoned Karna 78
  Chapter 39: Vyasa Explains the Incarnation of the Gods as
    Warriors 80
  Chapter 40: The Dead Warriors Appear out of the Ganges 82
  Chapter 41: The Returned Warriors Depart and Their
    Wives Enter the Ganges 83
  Chapter 44: The Pandavas Take Leave of Dhritarashtra,
    Gandhari, and Kunti 86
Part Three: The Arrival of Narada 90
  Chapter 45: Narada Arrives and Tells Yudhishthira How
    Dhritarashtra, Gandhari, and Kunti Died 90
  Chapter 46: Yudhishthira Mourns for the Dead and Curses
    Kingship 93
  Chapter 47: Narada Explains the Fire and Yudhishthira
    Performs the Funerals 95

Book Sixteen, *Mausala Parvan*, The Book of the Battle of the Clubs 98
  Preface to Book Sixteen 98

Chapter 1: Yudhishthira Sees Omens and Learns about
    the Battle of the Clubs 100
Chapter 2: The Sages Curse the Vrishnis and the
    Club Appears 101
Chapter 3: Evil Omens Appear and Krishna Proclaims a
    Pilgrimage 103
Chapter 4: The Vrishnis Go on a Pilgrimage and a
    Fight Breaks Out 105
Chapter 5: Krishna and Balarama Depart and Die 110
Chapter 6: Arjuna Goes to Dvaraka 114
Chapter 7: Arjuna Visits Vasudeva, Who Grieves and
    Vows to Die 116
Chapter 8: Arjuna Leads the Vrishni Women out of
    Dvaraka and Bandits Attack 118
Chapter 9: Arjuna Visits Vyasa and Yudhishthira 124

Book Seventeen, *Mahaprasthanika Parvan*, The Book of the Great Departure — 129

Preface to Book Seventeen 129
Chapter 1: The Pandavas Install the Kings, Depart,
    and Encounter Fire 130
Chapter 2: Draupadi, Sahadeva, Nakula, Arjuna,
    and Bhima Fall 134
Chapter 3: Yudhishthira Goes to Heaven, With a Dog 137

Book Eighteen, *Svargarohana Parvan*, The Book of Climbing to Heaven — 142

Preface to Book Eighteen 142
Chapter 1: Yudhishthira Reaches Heaven and Encounters
    Duryodhana 143
Chapter 2: Yudhishthira Goes to Hell and Meets His
    Brothers and Draupadi 145
Chapter 3: Yudhishthira Remains in Heaven and Bathes in
    the Heavenly Ganges 149
Chapter 4: Yudhishthira in Heaven Meets the Reborn
    Warriors from Both Sides 152
Chapter 5: Everyone Becomes the Gods They Always Were .. 154
Epilogue: The Fruits of Hearing the *Mahabharata* 156

Appendices 163

Appendix 1: Adjectives Applied to Several Characters 163
Appendix 2: Names and Epithets of Central Characters 165
Appendix 3: Minor Characters and Classes of Beings 169
Appendix 4: The Earlier Lives of the Protagonists of the
   Last Books of the *Mahabharata* 172
Appendix 5: Bibliography for Further Reading 175
Appendix 6: Technical Textual Notes 178

Acknowledgments

I've worked on the *Mahabharata* for many years, but most intensely during the last four years of my teaching at the University of Chicago, when I was privileged to teach the second quarter of second year Sanskrit, the heart of the basic three-year sequence, and to read the last books of the *Mahabharata* with my students. I put this manuscript together while teaching my very last class, and I am particularly indebted to the students in that class, from whom I learned so much: Brigid Boll, Danica Cao, Liam Frisk, Ria Gandhi, Nathan Katkin, Sricharan B. Sheshashai, Justin Smolin, Tapan Srivastava, and Benjamin Yusen. I owe even more to my last few brilliant teaching assistants, Nell Hawley, Itamar Ramot, and Josephine Brill, who tactfully endured my rather cavalier attitude to Sanskrit grammar and encouraged even my most far-fetched interpretations.

Introduction

Part I: The Text and the Story

A great deal has been written about the meaning of the *Mahabharata* as a whole, some by me,[1] but I do not aspire to add to it here.[2] Readers will find in Appendix 5: Bibliography for Further Reading a selected list of useful books about the *Mahabharata* and in Appendix 4 a succinct summary of the parts of the earlier plot that are referenced in the four final books. This Introduction will analyze key episodes in the final books in greater detail and will sketch the early lives of the main characters. It will also discuss some of the central concepts on which the final books depend and attempt to justify the decisions that I made in translating it from the Sanskrit.

I must note in passing that both the South Asian tradition of retelling episodes from the *Mahabharata*[3] and the European

---

[1] Wendy Doniger, "Violence in the *Mahabharata*" and "Dharma in the *Mahabharata*," in *The Hindus: An Alternative History* (New York: Penguin Press, 2009), pp. 252–304; "Women in the *Mahabharata*" and "The History of Ekalavya," in *On Hinduism* (Delhi: Aleph Book, 2013; 2nd edition, 2014; New York: Oxford University Press, 2014), pp. 537–559; and "Duty and Disaster in the *Mahabharata* of Vyasa (300 BCE to 300 CE)," in *Hinduism*, in *The Norton Anthology of World Religions*, edited by Jack Miles (New York: Norton, 2014), pp. 66–103.

[2] The best introduction to the text I know is W. J. Johnson's 1998 summary of the entire plot, with a wise analysis of the text as a whole: W. J. Johnson, *The Sauptikaparvan of the Mahabharata. The Massacre at Night. A New Verse Translation* (New York: Oxford University Press, 1998).

[3] An interesting exception to this generalization is a retelling of Book Eighteen, *Svargarohana*, by the fifteenth-century Hindi poet Vishnudas. It is included as an appendix beginning on page 325 of Haridar Dvivedi's edition of Vishnudas's *Pandavacarit* (Vidya Mandira Prakashana, 1973). I am indebted to Nell Hawley for this information.

scholarly tradition[4] have largely neglected the final books, perhaps because of their darkness and their unresolved ethical challenges. This neglect is, as I hope the reader will discover, most unjustified, underrating the high emotion, mythological inventiveness, metaphysical complexities, and conflicted characters that animate these books. Moreover, it is precisely the uncompromising and unresolved nature of their ethics that makes these books particularly useful to us in this age of doubt and confusion. I hope this brief introduction will show how important these final books are to the *Mahabharata* as a whole, how they not only confront many of the paradoxes of the earlier books but also tell a unified and self-bounded story of their own, and how wrong the native and scholarly traditions have been to neglect them.

The *Mahabharata* is a great poem that was composed in Sanskrit, the language of ancient India, probably in North India between approximately 300 BCE and 300 CE, though the central story had been told for centuries before that.[5] The Sanskrit *Mahabharata* that we have now is a text of about 75,000 verses (sometimes said to be 100,000, as the *Mahabharata* itself claims[6]), or about three million words, some fifteen times the combined length of the Hebrew Bible and the New Testament, or seven times the *Iliad* and the *Odyssey* combined. It was transmitted first orally, then in manuscripts, then in both ways, for many centuries, flickering back and forth between Sanskrit manuscripts and village storytellers, each adding new gemstones to the old mosaic, constantly reinterpreting it, until it

---

[4] An important exception is a recent book by Naama Shalom, who argues convincingly that the final book, Climbing to Heaven, is not only an intrinsic but also a crucial part of the text. Naama Shalom, *Re-ending The Mahabharata: The Rejection of Dharma in the Sanskrit Epic* (Albany: State University of New York Press, 2017).

[5] These dates are much disputed, some scholars emphasizing a much shorter period for the actual recension, with the possibility of single authorship, while others emphasize the longer period and multiple authorship. See Doniger, *The Hindus*, pp. 261–263.

[6] This statement is made at 1.56.13. But some manuscripts insert, after 18.5.40 (q.v.), a more qualified claim, that the 100,000-verse version is the one abbreviated for humans, the equivalent of what we might regard as the *Reader's Digest* version; much longer versions are found among the gods and other supernatural creatures.

was edited in a critical edition between 1933 and 1969 in Pune. That is the edition translated here.[7]

The name *Mahabharata* is often said to mean "The Great [Story of the] Bharatas" or "The Great [War of the] Bharatas," *maha* being cognate with the Latin *magna* and the Greek *mega*, and Bharata the name of the ancient ancestor of the heroes of the story. The text itself says, "It is called the *Mahabharata* because it tells of the great birth (*mahajjanma*) of the Bharatas."[8] Though we tend, Eurocentrically, to call it an epic, because of its resemblance, in many ways, to the ancient Greek Homeric epics, the Indians call it a history, an *itihasa*, literally "that [which has just been said] is what happened."[9] The text sings of the great Mahabharata war, which is sometimes supposed to have occurred between 1000 and 400 BCE,[10] sometimes in 3012 BCE or 950 BCE. That fraternal war was fought between the two branches of the Bharatas, the sons of Pandu and Dhritarashtra, called the Pandavas and the Kauravas.[11]

The story is set in and around the city of Hastinapura (now generally called Hastinapur), "The City of the Elephant," already a great city by 1000 BCE.[12] Most of the action takes place in the area between the upper Ganges River and the Yamuna River; some of it south of Hastinapur in the city of Indraprastha, "Indra's

---

[7] *Mahabharata*, for the first time critically edited by Vishnu S. Sukthankar, S. K. Belvalkar, et al. (Poona: Bhandarkar Oriental Research Institute, 1933–1969).

[8] This verse first occurs at 1.56.31 and is then inserted after 18.5.37 by several manuscripts: K3–5, B, Dn, D1–3, 7–9, Ts and the Bombay edition. See Appendix 6.

[9] 18.5.31.

[10] Hermann Kulke and Dietmar Rothermund, *A History of India* (London: Routledge, 1986), p. 45.

[11] "Kaurava" technically designates anyone from either side of the family, all of whom are descended from both Bharata and a king named Kuru, though the term is usually applied to the descendants of Dhritarashtra, as against the descendants of Pandu, the Pandavas. "Kaurava" is often used as an epithet for Dhritarashtra but not usually for anyone else.

[12] Romila Thapar, *Early India: From the Origins to 1300* (London: Penguin, 2002; Berkeley: University of California Press, 2004), p, 139; Kunal Chakravarti, *Themes in Indian History*, Oxford Readings in Sociology (Delhi: Oxford University Press, 2006), p. 74B.

Place,"[13] the Pandava capital, where present-day Delhi is situated; or in the Punjab, which the text refers to as the Land of Five Rivers ("*punj/panch*" meaning "five" and "ab/ap" meaning "water"). Kurukshetra (The Field of the Kurus), in what is now the district of Haryana, is where the battle took place,[14] and the city of Dvaraka, in Gujarat on the shore of the Arabian Sea, plays a part in the story until the ocean floods it.[15]

The *Mahabharata* was like an ancient Wikipedia, to which anyone who knew Sanskrit, or who knew someone who knew Sanskrit, could add a bit here, a bit there. But the powerful intertextuality of India ensured that anyone who added anything to the *Mahabharata* was well aware of the whole textual tradition behind it and fitted their own insight, or story, thoughtfully into the ongoing conversation. However diverse its sources, for several thousand years the tradition has regarded it as a coherent conversation among people who know one another's views and argue with silent partners. The contradictions in the text are sometimes the result of the self-indulgence of a rogue bard or the mistakes of a sloppy editor, but often they signal enduring cultural dilemmas that no author could ever have resolved. The text has an integrity that the culture supports and that it is our duty to acknowledge.

The *Mahabharata* is divided into eighteen books, called *parvans* (sections). After the first book, which provides a prelude and background, the rest fall into two more or less equal halves: the war (with its attendant preludes, myths, arguments, and subplots) occupies nine books (two through ten), while the last eight books (eleven through eighteen) describe the aftermath of the war. This second half begins with the mourning of the women (Book Eleven, The

---

[13] The text often puns on the name of both cities, substituting other words for "Elephant" or "City" or "Indra" or "Place," or all of the above.

[14] Kurukshetra is generally said to be south of the Punjab, north of Delhi, and east of the desert.

[15] Although there is no archeological evidence that the city of Dvaraka ever existed, from time to time someone tries to find traces of it in the waters off the west coast of India in the Arabian Sea. See Doniger, *The Hindus*, pp. 54–60.

Book of the Women [*Stri Parvan*]), to which it responds with philosophical teachings about the meaning (and meaninglessness) of life and death (Books Twelve, The Book of Peace [*Shanti Parvan*], and Thirteen, The Book of the Teachings [*Anushasana Parvan*]) and the celebration of a great ritual to atone for the evils of the war (Book Fourteen, The Book of the Horse Sacrifice [*Ashvamedhika Parvan*]).

Book Fifteen, The Book of Living in the Ashram (*Ashramavasika Parvan*), is divided into three parts. The first 25 chapters of Part One consist primarily of rather desultory arguments for and against a king's right to retire to the forest. The text from Chapter 26 deconstructs both the cautious triumphalism of Book Fourteen, The Book of the Horse Sacrifice (*Ashvamedhika Parvan*), and the piety of the first half of Book Fifteen. My translation takes up the final thread where the action begins, at Chapter 26 in Part One, the point where the old King Dhritarashtra finally retires to the forest. In fact, Part Two of Book Fifteen doubles back to begin again precisely where Chapter 26 of Part One began, as if to acknowledge that that point, Chapter 26, and not Chapter 1, is where the story really begins. This is another justification (in addition to the static quality of the first 25 verses) for beginning this translation there rather than at the start of Book Fifteen.

The Older Generation: The Birth of Pandu, Dhritarashtra, and Vidura

One way that the tradition affirms the unity of the *Mahabharata* is by attributing it to a single author, Vyasa (though his name just means "the Arranger" rather than "the Author"). Vyasa is also a major player in the story; he is both the author of the story of the heroes (the Pandavas and Kauravas) and the author of the Pandavas and Kauravas themselves, a combination of epic poet and walking sperm bank. His birth involves a confusion of the four ancient Indian classes that were supposed, ideally, never to be confused: Brahmin (the highest class, the class of priests, also called the Twice-born[16]), Kshatriya (kings and warriors), Vaishya (merchants and farmers), and Shudra (servants). This is how the story goes:

> Satyavati, the daughter of a king and a fish [it's a long story], was seduced by the Brahmin sage Parashara (who repaid her by removing her fishy smell) and gave birth on an island to the sage Vyasa, whom she abandoned. Later, Satyavati married King Shantanu and gave birth to another son, Vichitravirya, who became king but died childless, leaving two widows, the Kshatriya princesses Ambika and Ambalika.[17] Satyavati, who did not want the lineage to end, summoned her first son, the Brahmin sage, Vyasa, to father children on behalf of his dead half-brother, King Vichitravirya, posthumously.
>
> Vyasa was ugly and foul-smelling; his beard was red, his hair orange. Because Ambika closed her eyes when she conceived her son, Vyasa cursed him to be born blind: he was Dhritarashtra. Ambalika turned pale and so conceived Pandu the Pale. When Vyasa was sent to Ambika a second time, she sent in her place a Shudra servant girl, who gave birth to a healthy son, Vidura.[18]

The Levirate (*niyoga*) is the law by which a brother (or, sometimes, any male in the family[19]) begets legal children on behalf of his dead or impotent brother--or, as the Sanskrit puts it, sows his seed in the field

---

[16] The term "Twice-born" more precisely refers to the first three classes, all of whose male members are reborn at their coming-of-age ceremony. But in many texts, including the *Mahabharata*, the term usually refers only to Brahmins.

[17] The arrangement was originally more symmetrical, for there had been a third woman, Amba, but she departed before Vyasa arrived on the scene; eventually, she caused other complicated disasters that need not concern us here. Amba is clearly the basic name, of which Ambika and Ambalika are variants.

[18] 1.95–100.

[19] *Arthashastra* of Kautilya, ed. and trans. R. P. Kangle. Vol. 1: Text. Vol. 2: Translation, (Bombay: University of Bombay, 1960), 3.4.27–41. In fact, often it is said to be sufficient to call on any Brahmin to act on behalf of the dead man.

of the dead man.[20] The Levirate, though allowed by Hindu law, often, as here, miscarries.[21] In this disastrous Levirate, two of the three sons (Dhritarashtra and Pandu) have for great-grandparents a female fish, two Brahmins, and five Kshatriyas, while the third (Vidura) has a Kshatriya, a female fish, two Brahmins, and four Shudras.

The widows reject Vyasa because he is old and ugly and smells fishy (a characteristic that he apparently took from his mother when she lost it). He is also the wrong color, and this, plus the temporary pallor of the woman forced to conceive by him, results in the birth of a child, Pandu, who is the wrong color—"Pale," perhaps an albino, perhaps sickly, perhaps a euphemism for his future impotence. At the moment of conception, Dhritarashtra's mother-to-be closes her eyes (and, presumably, thinks of Hastinapur), and so her son is blind. The two princesses' recoiling from Vyasa produces physical disabilities in their sons—blindness and pallor—that cast shadows on those sons' claims to the kingship. The third mother, the slave girl, though she does not resist Vyasa in any way, produces a son, Vidura, who is disqualified because of his low, mixed class (the son of a Brahmin or Kshatriya father and Shudra mother), and who has no descendants; he attends his brothers as a wise counselor, a kind of attendant (called a *Kshattri*).

But there is yet another story behind the birth of Vidura. It involves Dharma, who is, in the *Mahabharata,* both a moral principle (lower case dharma) and a god (upper case Dharma). Dharma the god is called to account for his mistakes; for even Dharma has *karma* (a word that means both one's actions and the moral result of one's actions), and in this case his mistake leads to his being born as a human, Vidura:

> There was once a Brahmin named Mandavya, an expert on dharma, who had kept a vow of silence for a long time. One day,

---

[20] 15.35.15.
[21] Wendy Doniger, *The Bedtrick: Tales of Sex and Masquerade* (Chicago: University of Chicago Press, 2000), pp. 248–254.

robbers hid in his house, and when he refused to break his vow to tell the police where they were, and the police then found the robbers hiding there, the king passed judgment on Mandavya along with the thieves: "Kill him." The executioners impaled him on a stake. The Brahmin, whose very soul was dharma, remained on the stake for a long time. Though he had no food, he did not die, for he had great *tapas* [a kind of supernatural power manifest as heat]; he willed his life's breaths to remain within him, until the king came to him and said, "Greatest of sages, please forgive me for the mistake that I made in my delusion and ignorance." The sage forgave him, and the king had him taken down from the stake.

But then Mandavya went to the house of Dharma and scolded him, saying, "What did I do, without knowing what I had done, something so bad that it earned me such retribution?" Dharma said, "You stuck blades of grass up the tails of little butterflies when you were a child, and this [Mandavya's impalement on a stake that penetrated upward from the anus] is the fruit of that *karma*." Then Mandavya said, "For a rather small offense you have given me an enormous punishment. Because of that, Dharma, you will be born as a man, in the womb of a Shudra. And I will establish a moral boundary for the fruition of dharma in the world: no crime will be counted against anyone until the age of fourteen."[22]

That the Brahmin who knows dharma is mightier than the king should not surprise anyone familiar with these texts, which are, after all, generally composed by Brahmins. But that a man who was impaled on a stake like a common criminal is mightier even than the god Dharma is worthy of note. The moral law is stupid—children should not be so cruelly punished for their mischief, even when it involves cruelty to insects—and so the moral law must undergo its own expiation. Dharma, the god, must undergo the curse for the miscarriage of dharma, the moral principle.

[22] 1.101.

The Birth of the Sons of Pandu and Kunti

The *Mahabharata* goes on to tell us how, in the next generation, Pandu was cursed to die if he ever mated with any of his wives because he had come upon a man who had taken the form of a stag to mate with his wife/doe, and Pandu had killed the stag before he could consummate the mating.[23] Fortunately, Pandu's wife, Kunti, had a *mantra* that allowed her to invoke gods as proxy fathers of Pandu's sons. She invoked Dharma (who fathered Yudhishthira), the Wind (Vayu, father of Bhima), and Indra (king of the gods, father of Arjuna).[24] In addition to Dharma's two different paternal connections (with Vidura and Yudhishthira), Dharma continues to exist as a moral principle and is also able to appear on earth as the god Dharma (first in disguise, and then as himself) when he tests his son Yudhishthira on three occasions, the last two of which occur after Vidura has died and merged with Yudhishthira (and Dharma).[25]

Kunti then generously lent her *mantra* to Madri, Pandu's second wife, who invoked the Ashvins (twin equine gods, the Indian cousins of the Dioskouroi and Gemini) to father the twins, Nakula and Sahadeva. Years later, Pandu seduced Madri when he was overcome by desire for her; he died, in fulfillment of the stag's curse and in imitation of the stag's death: a fatal *coitus interruptus*, the sweet death transformed into a bitter death.

But Kunti had already had one son, secretly, out of wedlock: when she was still a young girl, she had decided to try out her *mantra*, just fooling around. The Sun god, Surya, took her seriously; despite her vigorous protests and entreaties, he raped her and afterward restored her virginity. She gave birth to Karna, whom she abandoned; a husband and wife of the low caste of Sutas (a combination of charioteer and bard, therefore a polluting mix of Kshatriya and

[23] 1.90.64; 1.109.5–30.
[24] 1.90, 1.101.
[25] 15.33.

Brahmin) adopted him and raised him as their own.[26] Karna is in many ways a shadow of Vidura. Where Vidura is an incarnate god, raised royally but treated as a half-caste (a Kshattri), and has both a Brahmin surrogate father (Vyasa in place of King Vichitravirya) and a low-caste surrogate mother (the maid in place of Ambika), Karna is of royal birth but is raised as a person of low class; he has a divine father (Surya), a royal mother (Kunti), and two low-class surrogate parents (the Sutas).

The Marriage of Draupadi

Draupadi is the wife of all five of the Pandavas. The authors of the *Mahabharata*, apparently troubled by this departure from normal ancient Indian marriage customs, offer several different excuses (always a cause for suspicion). First, the text says that Arjuna won Draupadi in a contest and brought her home to present her to his mother; as he and his brothers approached the house, they called out, "Look what we got!" and Kunti, not looking up, said, as any good mother would, "Share it together among all of you."[27] And so all five brothers married Draupadi. Not content with this rather far-fetched explanation, the *Mahabharata* tries again: Vyasa says that all five Pandavas are really incarnations of Indra (which does not contradict the statement that only Arjuna was the *son* of Indra, since, as we have seen, these are two different processes) and Draupadi is the incarnation of Shri (the goddess of prosperity, the wife of Indra and of all kings). And so, *sub specie aeternitatis*, Draupadi really had only one husband.[28]

---

[26] 1.104, 3.290–294, 5.144, 11.27, 15.38. Sanjaya, Dhritarashtra's companion, is also a Suta.
[27] 1.182.
[28] 1.189.1–40; cf. 15.39.1–15.

Still not satisfied, Vyasa offers a third explanation:

> The daughter of a great sage longed in vain for a husband; she pleased the god Shiva, who offered her a boon, and she asked for a virtuous husband. But in her eagerness she asked again and again, five times, and so Shiva said, "You will have *five* virtuous husbands." And that is why she married the five Pandavas.[29]

This mythological revisionism was not sufficient to protect Draupadi from frequent slurs against her presumed promiscuity. Yet all of her five sons are legitimate; they are called the Draupadeyas, "Draupadi's sons," a matronymic that cannily avoids the necessity of five different patronymics.[30] So, too, the three triply-fathered sons of the divinely polyandrous Kunti (also called Pritha) are often called Kaunteyas or Parthas, "Children of Kunti," although they are also called Pandavas (along with Madri's two sons) because they have a single legitimate, if not natural, father, Pandu.

Draupadi had begun her life in fire: she is born out of her father's fire altar and has no mother.[31] But, unlike the many women in the *Mahabharata* who end their lives on their husband's funeral pyre, Draupadi does not die by fire, because (a) she dies (just) before her husbands, and in any case (b) none of them *have* funeral pyres—all six walk into heaven[32] at the end of the story.[33]

---

[29] 1.189.42–48.

[30] They are Prativindhya, son of Yudhishthira; Sutasoma, son of Bhima; Shrutakirti or Shrutakarman, son of Arjuna; Shatanika, son of Nakula; and Shrutasena, son of Sahadeva.

[31] 1.155.1–51. See the explanation of her divine nature at 18.4.9–10.

[32] The word that I am translating throughout as "heaven" is *svarga*, which literally means "going to the light" or "going to the sun." It might be translated better, though more cumbersomely, as "the celestial world" or even "the world of the gods." S*varga* is often explicitly contrasted with *naraka*, an underworld; there are a number of different underworlds (some made of water, some of fire, and some said to be evil-smelling places of torment) as well as different heavens (some inhabited by gods, some more metaphysically conceived). But since, in the *Mahabharata*, *svarga* and *naraka* are heavily moralized and explicitly contrasted, I thought it best to translate them as "heaven" and "hell," despite the Christian overtones of those words.

[33] 17.2, 18.2.

When the five Pandava brothers lost their kingdom to their cousins in a crooked game of dice, they went into exile with Draupadi for thirteen years, at the end of which they regained their kingdom through a cataclysmic war in which almost everyone on both sides was killed. It is at this point that the final books, translated here, take over, to follow our heroes through the tragic consequences of their Pyrrhic victory.

Grim as these passages are, they are occasionally relieved by episodes of humor. The contrast between life in the palace and life in the forest is satirized in the ludicrous disparity between poor old Dhritarashatra, trying to slip away into the woods to meditate in peace and quiet, and his nephew Yudhishthira, helpfully coming after Dhritarashtra with all of his brothers and a great army and truckloads of courtesans and gold bullion. (Dhritarashtra does give some of the gold to the hermits, but do they want it?[34]) This tension is then expressed in what I read as a satire on the excessively polite, formulaic questions that the rules of formal discourse dictate when two important people meet after a long absence, in this case a royal uncle and nephew. The slyly implied criticism of the royal life in the empty formalities of the old King Dhritarashtra's questions to his nephew Yudhishthira, making sure he's still running the kingdom properly, are met by the equally sly implied criticism of the forest life in Yudhishthira's pointed questions to Dhritarashtra, making sure everyone in his entourage is enjoying the austerities of life in the forest. And each of them cleverly avoids answering the other's questions at all.[35] The fact that Yudhishthira's questions to Dhritarashtra are soon repeated almost verbatim by Narada, as well as that once again they remain unanswered,[36] confirms that they are largely formal, as indeed they are explicitly said to be.[37]

---

[34] 15.30, 34.
[35] 15.33.
[36] 15.35.2–6.
[37] 15.32.18.

INTRODUCTION 13

There is also humor in the character of the busybody sage Narada, who always insists that he has seen with his own eyes any event that he narrates[38] and always arrives at the crucial moment "by chance."[39] Other wandering sages, too, are treated with respect but are also depicted as self-important, hot-tempered buffoons. Often these sages (particularly Narada) act as the grain of sand in the oyster, the unexpected factor that makes the plot take the turn it needs to take.[40]

Part II: The Last Books of the *Mahabharata*

Most of the men in the first half of the *Mahabharata* die in battle, but the four final books explore other ways in which people choose to abandon life on earth. Their mental agony leads some of them, particularly but not only the oldest, to withdraw into a denial of normal sensual functions, at first turning away from sexuality, then from almost all food, and ultimately shutting down and erasing all human needs. Vidura somehow merges into the body of the still living Yudhishthira,[41] a haunting embodiment of the belief that the dead somehow remain part of us after they die, as we suddenly hear the voice of our dead brother in our own words or see him in the way we walk. Some women plunge into the Ganges in order to join their husbands in heaven.[42] A few of the young men start drinking and lose their tempers and die in a drunken brawl that eventually kills almost all the men in the family.[43] Krishna's brother Balarama turns back into a snake (it's a long story) and plunges into the ocean, and Krishna is fatally wounded, in his Achilles heel, by

---

[38] 15.26.5.
[39] 15.26.9, 15.27.8, 15.45.1, 15.45.35, etc.
[40] It is Narada who blurts out the information that makes Yudhishthira realize that his brothers are not in heaven, precipitating his decision to leave heaven (17.3.25–29).
[41] 15.33.
[42] 15.41.
[43] 16.4.

a hunter with the improbable name of Old Age.[44] Krishna's father simply quietly stops breathing.[45] Finally, the five Pandava brothers and their wife leave earth by climbing up to an afterlife first in hell and then in heaven (Book Seventeen), where some of them are surprised (and very sorry indeed) to encounter their earthly enemies (Book Eighteen).

Book Fifteen (Living in the Ashram) and Book Eleven (The Women)

The final books have specific roots in earlier parts of the second half of the *Mahabharata*. The Book of the Women (Book Eleven, *Stri Parvan*) comes right after the Book of the Night Raid (Book Ten, *Sauptika Parvan*), the last, most grotesque, and most mythological of the battle books. The women in Book Eleven, reacting to that final sordid bloodbath, express the human tragedy of the whole war. The books that follow, Books Twelve, Thirteen, and Fourteen, offer different responses to questions posed by the women, primarily philosophical and religious attempts to make sense of the carnage, ideological balm for the women's psychic wounds. Book Fifteen (Living in the Ashram, *Ashramavasika*) then narrates fifteen years of peaceful rule by the Pandavas, until they once again become disconsolate and return to the questions raised in Book Eleven: again the women mourn, and in particular Gandhari mourns for her dead sons and Kunti mourns for her abandoned son, Karna. Book Eleven therefore provides a significant prelude to the beginning of the portion of the text that concerns us in Book Fifteen.

In Book Eleven, when the women perform the libations for the dead in their family, Kunti insists that they perform the libations for Karna, too. When questions arise, since Karna has never been

---

[44] 16.5.
[45] 16.8.15.

regarded as a member of the family, Kunti simply says that Karna was her son, fathered by the Sun.[46] When Yudhishthira now learns that Kunti had kept secret the fact that Karna was her son, he berates her; if he had known that Karna was part of their branch of the family, he could have had Karna fight for them, and they would not have lost so many of their own men. (Yudhishthira is still very cross about this even in heaven, where he complains, "Not even Indra could have conquered us in battle if we had had Karna on our side"[47]). And so Yudhishthira curses all women to be forever unable to keep secrets. This is all that Kunti's revelation means to him. But Kunti grieves for her abandoned child again, and at much greater length, in Book Fifteen.

In contrast, Gandhari's grief in Book Eleven looks not to the past, as Kunti's does, but to the future, and it has serious consequences for the later books of the *Mahabharata*. Gandhari had amassed great *tapas* by covering her eyes in order to serve her blind husband, Dhritarashtra, faithfully all his life.[48] Then, in Book Nine (*Shalya Parvan*, The Book of Shalya), she is forestalled from cursing the Pandavas, in an episode that, significantly, involves a *club*: the Pandava Bhima had killed Duryodhana, one of Gandhari's sons, illegally, striking him below the belt with a club, breaking his thighs.[49] This misdeed eventually has serious fallout, in the Battle of the Clubs,[50] but it also has more immediate effects:

> Yudhishthira feared that when Gandhari learned how her son Duryodhana had been killed, she would use her *tapas* to destroy the Pandavas. And so Yudhishthira asked Krishna to go to Gandhari to quell her anger. Krishna reminded Gandhari that Duryodhana had disregarded her own warnings to him, and he

[46] 11.27.
[47] 18.2.8.
[48] 1.103.12–13.
[49] 9.57.
[50] 16.4.

concluded, "Don't ever set your mind on the destruction of the Pandavas. Of course, you are capable of burning up the entire earth, and all its creatures moving and unmoving, with your eye enflamed with anger by the power of your *tapas*. But do not do it." When she heard Krishna's words, Gandhari said, "Yes, let it be just as you say, Krishna."[51]

But Gandhari's fiery rage is only temporarily quelled. In Book Eleven, she becomes so angry with Yudhishthira that a flame from her eyes flashes out to destroy him, and only at the last minute does she rein it in so that it burns only his toenails.[52] But then she has a divine vision of the horrible battlefield with her hundred sons lying dead on the ground.[53] And when she sees this vision again, she seems to forget her promise to Krishna, and so she curses Krishna's clan, the Yadavas, descendant of Yadu, the large clan of which the Vrishnis and Bhojas and Andhakas are members:

> Gandhari fell to the ground, emaciated by grief, out of her mind with unhappiness, no longer able to hold herself together. Her whole body was suffused with anger, flooded by grief for her sons, all of her senses confused, and she laid the blame on Krishna:
>
> Gandhari said, "Krishna, the sons of Pandu and Dhritarashtra hated one another. Why did you look the other way when they were destroyed? You had the power, you had so many followers, you had a massive army, you had commitments to both sides, you heard what was said. You disregarded the destruction of the Kurus because you wanted it. And so you will now reap the reward for that. I amassed a certain amount of *tapas* by serving my husband, and I will curse you with that, though you are by nature so difficult to touch. Since you disregarded the Kurus and the

---

[51] 9.62.
[52] 11.15.
[53] 11.16.

Pandavas when they, kinsmen, were killing one another, you will kill your own kinsmen. When the thirty-sixth year from now has arrived, you will kill your relatives, kill your kinsmen, kill your family, and then you will wander in the woods until you yourself come to a contemptible end. And your wives—who will have seen their sons killed, and their families killed, and their kinsmen killed—will stagger about just as these wives of the Bharatas are doing now."

When he heard this horrible speech, the noble Krishna, smiling, said to Queen Gandhari, "My good woman, I and no one else will be the destroyer of the entire clan of the Vrishnis. I know this. Kshatriya woman, you are doing something that has already been done. *It is fated that the Vrishnis will be destroyed; there is no doubt about this.*[54] The Yadavas cannot be killed by other men or even by gods or anti-gods. And so they will destroy one another." When Krishna had said this, the minds of the Pandavas were shaken; they were deeply troubled and had no hope to live.[55]

Gandhari's tragic vision of the death of her sons is later balanced and, to some extent, exorcised by the vision of them all alive and well in heaven, a vision that will be granted to her in Book Fifteen. Book Fifteen answers the fires of cremation with the waters of funeral libations and balances the forest fire that kills Dhritarashtra and Gandhari with the water of the river out of which the dead warriors return to earth for a short visit. It offers magical solutions, visions of heaven, to the human problems of death and mourning.

But Gandhari's curse in Book Eleven will have its full effect in Book Sixteen, both in the deadly, drunken orgy and in Krishna's lonely death, like the death of an animal.

---

[54] Manuscripts K1.2, Dn1, D2.5, D.3 insert this sentence. See Appendix 6.
[55] 11.25.34–46.

Book Sixteen (The Battle of the Clubs), Gandhari's Curse, and Buddhist and Jain Variants

Book Sixteen, which begins when a boy dressed as a woman gives birth to an iron club, echoes another episode, this one from the beginning of the *Mahabharata*, in which Gandhari, after being pregnant for two years, brings forth from her womb a great mass "like an iron ball": she sprinkles it with water, and it fragments into a hundred pieces, which become the hundred (evil) sons of Gandhari and Dhritarashtra.[56] When all the sons born of that iron ball are killed in battle, Gandhari pronounces (in Book Eleven) the curse which ultimately (in Book Sixteen) results in the birth of the iron club that avenges the deaths of her sons born from the iron ball. The circle closes.

A different version of the origin of the club, minus Gandhari's curse and other details, is recorded in a Buddhist text:

> The Vrishnis dressed a boy up like a pregnant girl and teased Vyasa by asking him what she would deliver. The angry sage said that "she" would deliver a knot of Khadira wood. When that knot of wood was delivered, the Vrishnis ground it into powder and threw it into the river. The powder came together in a clump downstream and an *eraka* plant grew from it. In a fight, the Vrishnis struck each other with that plant's branches, which turned into clubs. The clan was thus destroyed.[57]

The boy pretending to be a pregnant girl, the weapon powdered in the river, the *eraka* grass, and the battle of clubs—all this also appears in the *Mahabharata* version of this episode. But in this Buddhist version, the club is not made of iron (as in the *Mahabharata*) but, more naturalistically, of wood, much more likely than iron to give

---

[56] 1.107.
[57] *Ghata Jataka*, no. 454 in *Jataka Stories*, ed. E. B. Cowell (London: Pali Text Society, 1973). The story is also more briefly retold in the *Samkicca Jataka*, no. 530.

rise to the growth of plants. Moreover, where the *Mahabharata* attributes the curse to a group of sages, the Buddhist text blames Vyasa himself.

Vyasa is also the villain (and Krishna and Balarama play an even more murderous role) in a version of the story told by the Jains in a text probably from the eighth century CE. The Jain text explains the role of wine (unexplained in the *Mahabharata* telling, which simply says that the warriors disregarded the king's decree forbidding them to drink and got drunk) but leaves out the pregnancy and the club. It also offers a version of Krishna's death slightly different from the version told in Book Sixteen of the *Mahabharata*:

> Balarama approached the Jina with his hands folded and said: "Everything that is created will also perish. So, how will Dvaraka meet its end? How will the city sink into the ocean?" The Jina, who sees everything, predicted that there would be a hermit called Vyasa who would cause the destruction of Dvaraka, and that a man called Jaratkumara ("Aging Youth") would mistake Krishna for a deer in the forest and cause his death.
>
> After the Yadavas returned to the city, their minds burning with misery, Krishna and Balarama commanded, "Bring out the wine!" Various types of liquor were prepared and consumed and then some was placed in a vessel and buried under the Kadamba Mountain. After this, Krishna announced to the Yadavas that everyone should renounce and should generate *tapas* with their minds on the Jina. Thus, many of the inhabitants of Dvaraka retired to the forest for many years to fast, generate *tapas*, and perform vows and rituals.
>
> After the rains had passed, Vyasa began to have false thoughts. He stood on a path near the Kadamba Mountain to generate *tapas*. One day, Samba and his friends were playing near Vyasa. They became thirsty and found the buried vessels of wine and began to drink it, thinking it to be water. Drunk on the wine, they changed: they became violent, their eyes turned red, and

they began to sing erratically. When they saw Vyasa, they recalled the Jina's words and realized, "This is that sage Vyasa who will cause the destruction of Dvaraka!" The princes began to beat Vyasa without any compassion until he fell to the ground, seething with anger and vowing to destroy the Yadavas. The news of Vyasa's anger quickly spread to the kingdom, where Krishna and Balarama ordered everyone to evacuate the city. They tried to calm Vyasa, but he resolved to burn down the entire city with its inhabitants. He did, however, raise two fingers, indicating to Balarama and Krishna that only they would escape his wrath.[58]

These Buddhist and Jain versions of the story omit some of the details in our text but include others that explain otherwise puzzling features. A good example of this is the strange use of the feminine noun *jara*, "Old Age," for the hunter in the *Mahabharata*. The masculine noun, *jaratkumara*, "Aging Youth," in the Jain text, makes much better sense, but is it the original reading or a Jain attempt to correct the more puzzling reading of the *Mahabharata*? In any case, the Buddhist and Jaina tellings may come from an ancient storytelling well from which all three of these great ancient Indian traditions drew different bits of the same story.[59]

Book Seventeen (The Great Departure) and Yudhishthira's Dog

Hindu dharma forbids Hindus to have any contact with dogs, which it regards as unclean scavengers, literally un-touchable (*a-sprishya*), the parasites of Dalits whom Hindus also regard as

---

[58] *Harivamsapurana* of Punnata Jinasena. Sanskrit Text with Hindi commentary, ed. Pannalal Jain (Varanasi: Bharathiya Jnanapitha, 1962) 61.16–69. My abridgement of a translation by Seema Chauhan, to whom I am greatly indebted.
[59] For more about this story, see Bruce M. Sullivan, *Krsna Dvaipayana Vyasa and the Mahabharata: A New Interpretation* (Leiden: E. J. Brill, 1994), pp. 102–107.

parasites. Yudhishthira uses dogs as symbols of aggression when he says that humans trying to negotiate peace are like dogs: "It starts with tails wagging, but then someone barks, and another barks back; they back off; they bare their teeth; they bark louder; then they fight, and the stronger one wins and wolfs down the meat. People are just exactly like that."[60] And even after he has won the war, Yudhishthira says: "We are not dogs, but we behaved like dogs ravenous for a piece of meat."[61]

A very different point of view appears in the episode in Book Seventeen in which a dog appears from nowhere shortly before Yudhishthira is about to enter heaven. Yudhishthira refuses to enter heaven without this stray dog who has attached himself to him. Strikingly, the god Dharma has become incarnate in this animal; eventually he resumes his own divine form. It is as if Jehovah in the Hebrew Bible had become incarnate in a pig. The text uses the dog to make a powerful ethical point; this is not, or not primarily, an argument for compassion for animals; rather, it is a way of arguing about the sorts of humans who should or should not go to heaven (a topic the *Mahabharata* addresses explicitly in the final book) or even, perhaps, by extension, about the castes who should or should not be allowed into temples.

Yudhishthira refuses to abandon a dog who is "devoted" (*bhakta*) to him. The dog, the loyal dog, is, after all, the natural *bhakta* of the animal kingdom; it's no accident that it is a dog and not, say, a cat, that follows Yudhishthira like that. (Cats, in Hinduism, are depicted as religious hypocrites.[62]) But *bhakti* at this period meant little more than belonging to someone, being dedicated to someone as a servant or loyal friend (or, occasionally a lover); it did not yet have the overtone of passionate love between a deity and a devotee that was to become characteristic of a branch of medieval Hinduism. As

---

[60] 5.70.70–72.
[61] 12.7.10.
[62] The hypocritical cat ascetic is carved on the great frieze at Mamallapuram. See Doniger, *On Hinduism*, pp. 51–52.

the word *bhakti* expanded its meaning, the story of Yudhishthira and his dog often came to be read as a model for that sort of devotion. Once we realize this connection, we see that *bhakti* binds the object of devotion to the devotee as much as it binds the devotee to the object of devotion. Yudhishthira *must* take the dog with him.

Indra's argument, that dogs would pollute the sacrificial offerings by looking at them or touching them, is a common one. The lawmaker Manu warns that if the king did not wield the rod of punishment justly, dogs would lick the oblation and everything would be topsy turvy.[63] In the *Mahabharata* version of the story of Rama and Sita, when Rama throws Sita out after her sojourn in Ravana's house, he compares her to an oblation that a dog has licked.[64] Much of the trouble in the *Mahabharata* begins with a dog that does *not* lick an oblation: when Janamejaya and his brothers were performing a sacrifice, a dog, offspring of the bitch Sarama, came near. The brothers beat the dog, who ran howling back to his mother and told her that they had beaten him though he had neither looked at nor licked the offerings. Sarama then went to the sacrificial grounds and said to Janamejaya, "Since you beat my son when he had not done anything wrong, danger will befall you when you do not see it coming."[65] As a result of his unjustified mistreatment of this pup, Janamejaya soon gets into serious trouble with other animals (snakes; it's a long story). Thus the *Mahabharata* both begins and ends with a story about justice for dogs.

The text here draws upon the Vedic (indeed, Indo-European) attitude to dogs. Sarama is the mother of the four-eyed brindled dogs who (like Cerberus in Greek mythology) guard the entrance to the afterworld, precisely where Yudhishthira encounters the dog here. Yudhishthira is often called "Dharmaraja," but so is Yama, the god of the dead, to whom the brindled hounds of hell belong.

---

[63] 7.21.
[64] 3.275.14.
[65] 1.3.1–18.

So, according to Vedic dharma, the dog does belong at the gate of heaven, but according to Hindu dharma, the dog cannot pass through that gate.

And so, in Yudhishthira's case the conflict remains unresolved; the text equivocates. It seems that the dog is part of a series of tests that Dharma has set for his son Yudhishthira, all of which he passes.[66] The dog never does go to heaven, never violates or challenges Hindu law, because there was no dog; it was all an illusion. The fact that the dog trots along at the *end* of the file of Pandavas should have alerted us from the start: what self-respecting dog ever went anywhere but at the *front* of a group of humans? Even in the *Rig Veda*, the bitch Sarama is a "path-finder."[67] And so this cannot be a real, card-carrying dog. And indeed, no dog gets into heaven in the *Mahabharata*. The story shows just how unfair (might one say "undharmic"?) the system is but does not change it.

"I am determined not to be cruel," says Yudhishthira. The word he uses for "not cruel," which occurs here four times in four verses,[68] is *anrishamsya*, which is often wrongly translated as "compassionate," though there is another, more positive Sanskrit word for compassion, *anukrosha*, "weeping for" or "weeping with," a vivid form of sym-pathy. The god Dharma later praises Yudhishthira for "weeping with" all creatures (*anukrosha*).[69] *Anrishamsya* is not so strong as *anukrosha*, merely indicating a disinclination to be cruel (*shamsya*) to humans (*nri*), much as *ahimsa* (often translated as "non-injury," more precisely, "lack of a desire to harm") indicates a disinclination to injure, rather than an active desire to be merciful.

"Not cruel" is a doubly weakened word: a double negative (it doesn't refer to doing something good, just to not doing something bad) and species specific (referring only to harm to humans). To

---

[66] 17.3.18.
[67] *Rig Veda* 3.31.6. See Wendy Doniger O'Flaherty, *The Rig Veda: An Anthology* (London: Penguin Books, 1981), p. 151. See also *Rig Veda* 10.108, p 156.
[68] 17.3.7, 8, 10, and 30.
[69] 17.3.16.

apply it to the treatment of an animal is therefore rather forced, given the usual Hindu distinction between the status and treatment of humans and of animals. Yudhishthira is damning himself with faint praise if all he can muster up, in place of either "compassion" or "weeping with," is that he doesn't harm humans. He is hedging. Yudhishthira's dharmic behavior passes the test, but the issue of dogs in heaven is never resolved. Bhakti presents dharma with a challenge, which dharma parries without actually yielding.

Book Eighteen (Climbing to Heaven) and the Transfer of *Karma*

That even Dharma has *karma*, as we saw in the tale of Mandavya and Vidura, is an indication of how powerful a force *karma* had become by this time in India. The *Mahabharata* teeters on the brink of a full-fledged concept of the transfer of *karma* in a passage that takes up the story after Yudhishthira has entered heaven and then turned back and gone down to hell. Yudhishthira's ability to ease his brothers' torments in hell takes the form of a cool, sweet breeze that counteracts the hot, putrid air of hell, through a kind of transfer of merit, ultimately a transfer of *karma*.[70] He therefore wants to stay with his brothers in hell, even though he himself does not belong there, just as he wanted to stay with the dog outside heaven, again where he did not belong. Elsewhere in the *Mahabharata*, when a king wants to take over the guilt of his priest in hell (an interesting role reversal: the priest in this incident had sacrificed a child so that the king could get a hundred sons), Dharma protests, "No one ever experiences the fruit of another person's *karma*." The king,

---

[70] There is a rough parallel to this idea in the Catholic practice of offering up one's suffering to shorten the sentence of souls in purgatory. Thanks to David Tracy for this insight. See also Wendy Doniger O'Flaherty, "Karma and Rebirth in the Vedas and Puranas," pp. 1–39 of *Karma and Rebirth in Classical Indian Traditions*, ed. Wendy Doniger O'Flaherty (Berkeley: University of California Press,; Delhi, Motilal Banarsidass, 1980; University of Chicago Press, 2018).

however, insists on living in hell along with the priest for the same term, and eventually both he and the priest go to heaven.[71] The king does not save the priest from suffering, but he suffers with him—sym-pathy, which is to say, *anukrosha*. In the case of Yudhishthira in hell, no one tries to persuade him to leave; they learned how stubborn he was the last time, with the dog at the gates of heaven. What, then, is the solution? A sure sign of a moral impasse in any narrative is the invocation of the "it was just a dream" motif at the end, erasing the *aporia* entirely. Another is the deus ex machina. The *Mahabharata* invokes both here, a double red flag. The gods appear and explain that, as Yudhishthira had once told an illusory lie, so he has had only an illusory experience of hell. The darkness of hell vanishes, and Yudhishthira finds himself in heaven. But he is still not convinced that the system is just, and he reviles the gods and their dharma.[72]

The commentator Vadiraja Tirtha, in the sixteenth century, explained how it was that the darkness in hell suddenly disappeared:[73]

> When Krishna had told Yudhishthira to say to Drona, "Ashvatthaman has been killed" [truthfully referring to a dead elephant named Ashvatthaman but apparently, and misleadingly, referring to Drona's living son Ashvatthaman], Yudhishthira, not trusting Krishna [and with good reason], added, under his breath, "The elephant."[74] Even though Yudhishthira committed no deception by saying, "Ashvatthaman has been killed," because he said, secretly, "The elephant," Krishna's words made Yudhishthira aware that there had been a deception.[75] That combination of

---

[71] 3.128.
[72] 18.2.50.
[73] 18.3.3.
[74] 7.164.160.
[75] Nilakantha says that Drona had been deceived about the death of Ashvatthaman; the deception was covered up by the word "elephant," announcing that the reference was to someone other than a human.

truth and falsehood made it necessary for Yudhishthira to see hell for just a short time, and the gods fabricated a special hell for that purpose.[76] But this contradicts what Indra had told Yudhishthira earlier: "You will see your brothers..."[77] So, when he met them in hell, and they said, "I am Bhima, I am Karna," and so forth, even though they were still alive, that was all fabricated by the gods. If it were real, how could one see the road to heaven [which is above the earth] in hell, which is below the earth? And so this passage does not contradict the statement, "When the assembled gods had arrived there, that darkness disappeared."[78]

But the "illusion" cop-out—it wasn't really hell, just as it wasn't really a dog—is belied by the perceived need for people to expiate their sins in a real hell. At this point the text introduces a discourse that cleverly unites what originally must have been quite distinct theories of the afterlife. The first is the earlier, Vedic theory, more precisely an Indo-European theory now perhaps best known from the depiction of Valhalla in Richard Wagner's Ring Cycle. According to this theory, good people, more precisely good warriors, when they die go to a vaguely understood heaven (and bad people go to an even more vaguely understood hell). The second theory is the later, Vedantic or Upanishadic, idea that the sum and balance of our good and bad deeds, our complex *karma*, determine the complex form of our rebirth on earth, except for those lucky few who achieve *moksha*, freedom from the cycle of rebirth. The term *moksha* appears in this part of the *Mahabharata* just once, to refer simply to dying, free from this earthly life, and going to a conventional heaven, with no suggestion of freedom from rebirth.[79] It is the earlier theory, the Valhalla theory, that dominates the last books of the *Mahabharata*; though there are numerous

[76] 18.2.14–25.
[77] 17.3.5.
[78] 18.3.3.
[79] 15.41.21.

references to rebirths on earth and, for the virtuous, eventually in heaven, there is almost nothing here about release from the cycle of rebirth.[80]

All through these final books, people wonder "what worlds" their beloved dead have gone to, implying a variety of possibilities. The king to whom the story is told in the frame (discussed later) first asks the narrator, "When the sons of Pandu and Dhritarashtra got to heaven, what positions did they enjoy?"[81] Later he asks about their "final destinations" or "levels of existence" (*gatis*), that is, the various sorts of lives into which they might have been reborn: "How long did the Pandavas remain in heaven? Or did they perhaps have a place there that would last forever? Or, at the end of their *karma*, what final destination did they reach?"[82]

A tentative answer is supplied by Nilakantha, who commented on the *Mahabharata* in the seventeenth century CE.[83] He begins by stating that, when each warrior went to heaven, he went to whatever god he had been a portion of. Some people unite right away with the deity of which they are a portion, while others unite after some time; yet others reach higher and higher ground and higher and higher levels of existence until, in the end, they may be freed from rebirth. And the *Mahabharata*'s reference to worlds "beyond which there is nothing," along with the fact that the Pandavas are not said to be reborn in earth, implies that their *karma* did eventually come to an end, in worlds that are the equivalent of *moksha*. Yet they may have suffered and rejoiced through eons and eons of their good and bad deeds, in real and unreal heavens and hells, before they reached that point.

---

[80] Despite its relative absence from the last books, there is a great deal about *moksha* elsewhere in the *Mahabharata*, including an entire long section called the *Moksha-parvan*. But in the final book, *moksha* is explicitly mentioned only once, at 18.5.38, at the very end of the whole text.

[81] 18.1.1.

[82] 18.5.1–6, 7bc, 8.

[83] *Mahabharata*, with the commentary of Nilakantha (Bombay: Jagadishvara, 1862). In my footnotes to the text I have occasionally included useful suggestions from Nilakantha.

The *Mahabharata* wants to have its *karma* and eat it too. It tells us that we all go both to heaven and to hell (in an order that seems counterintuitive: sinners first to heaven, virtuous people first to hell, although there is a logic in having the shorter stay come first in both cases). And then, although throughout its eighteen books it has told us that people (including gods) are reborn on earth as a result of their good and bad *karma*, it now tells us that, ultimately, we go beyond earth and beyond heaven and hell to—a place that cannot be described. The authors of the *Mahabharata* are thinking out loud, still trying to work it all out. They are keeping their minds open, refusing to reach a final verdict on a subject—the complex function of *karma*—on which the jury is still out.

Part III: The Meaning of the End of the Story

Death and Transfiguration

This is the story of people who survived the great disaster and couldn't bear to go on living any more when their friends and family were gone. Nilakantha (on 17.1.2) describes them as "those who have done what was to be done, but have been swallowed up by unbearable unhappiness." Particularly poignant is the mourning of parents—and, more particularly, the mourning of women, especially mothers who have lost their sons and husbands in the war. The ease with which so many people in the *Mahabharata* leave their lives on earth is explained by the prospect of what it is they believe they are going to. This vision of an afterlife is, as we have seen, complex, morally and mythologically rich, theologically deep, messy, inconsistent—in a word, full of life. What distinguishes heaven from life on earth is primarily the higher ethical code of its inhabitants, which might imply that a person who wants to get to heaven should try to live by that code on earth. Nilakantha states that Vyasa's aim was "to show the virtues that cause one to go to heaven and the faults that keep one from going to heaven."[84]

The problem, as the *Mahabharata* presents it, lies not in dying but in dying for the wrong reason or in the wrong way. Since this is a heroic epic, a martial epic, it generally views dying in battle as a Good Thing. But to die in battle ignominiously, to die in the act of killing people one should not kill, or killing them in the wrong way, is not a Good Thing. Many of the battle deaths are unheroic, and they trouble the killers in the aftermath of the war.[85] So, too, the death of Abhimanyu, just a young boy, all alone at the hands of a group of seasoned soldiers when his older companions failed to keep their promise to protect him, is a constant thorn in their side.[86] The heroes' surviving parents share these sorrows and have others of their own. King Dhritarashtra is haunted by the guilt of having failed to prevent his wicked son, Duryodhana, from waging the fratricidal war against Pandu's five sons in the first place and of having continued to refuse to stop Duryodhana (though many people urged him to do so) at various moments when it might have been possible.[87]

The women who mourn their sons and husbands are generally not so troubled by these strategic questions of Geneva convention/ Marquess of Queensbury violations; they simply grieve. But the two great mothers, Dhritarashtra's wife Gandhari and Pandu's widow Kunti, grieve in special ways that have consequences for the deaths and afterlives of the male heroes. Gandhari curses the men who had killed her sons and survived the war;[88] as we have seen, she curses them to die in a strangely convoluted way many years after the war.[89] Kunti's grief is quite different: many years after the war, she regrets the loss of her child years before the war, when, in violation

[84] On 17.1.2.
[85] 16.4.17–26.
[86] The episode is told at 7.47–38 and referred to at 15.28.12, 15.32.14, 15.37.8, 15.39.13.
[87] 15.36.
[88] 11.25.
[89] 16.3.19.

of dharma, she gave birth to a son—the tragic hero, Karna—whom she abandoned, also in violation of dharma.[90] This abandonment of her son was the woman's equivalent of a man's sin in killing another man in battle in violation of the rules of dharma (which also happens to Karna, whom Arjuna murders in violation of the ethics of battle[91]). Kunti's painful recollection of her treatment of Karna torments her repeatedly in the aftermath of the war, until finally the sage Vyasa grants her absolution: he reassures her that she was guiltless in yielding to the Sun god and abandoning Karna. He justifies his argument by assuring Kunti that she had no choice but to submit to the rape because the gods are totally amoral: "The dharma of humans has no connection with the dharma of the gods. You should understand this, Kunti, and let the fever in your mind vanish. Everything is within bounds for those who have brute power; everything is pure for those who have power. Everything is dharma for those who have power; everything of those who have power is their own."[92] This is a stunningly cynical attitude both to the gods and to what humans are taught to believe is the basis of their own moral action.

When Dhritarashtra and the two queens finally die, there is yet another sort of dilemma about a good death versus a bad death, this time hinging on the nature of the forest fire in which they die. It appears to be a random fire of no religious significance, hence the agent of an ignominious, meaningless death, the equivalent, for a Homeric warrior, of being left unburied as carrion for the birds and dogs to eat. But the sage Narada goes to great, if ultimately unconvincing, lengths to persuade the descendants of the dead king and queens that the fire was actually a consecrated, sacred, ritual fire, which would mean that they did not die profanely; and eventually their bones are recovered, and they are given a proper funeral.[93]

---

[90] 1.104, 3.290–294, 5.144, 11.27, 15.38.
[91] 8.66–67.
[92] 15.38.22–23.
[93] 15.47.

The idea that the source of the forest fire was in fact a sacrificial fire, then we may read it as an example of another important and recurrent *Mahabharata* metaphor: the war as a broken sacrifice or uncompleted sacrifice, a sacrifice that goes horribly wrong.

Theodicy and the Cause of Devastating War

In addition to the justification of individual deaths, the text returns again and again to the question of the justification for the destruction of almost all the Bharatas in the war and its aftermath. There are too many different explanations for that catastrophe; Freud would have called it overdetermined: it had to happen because of the gods' intervention, because of the perversity of time, because of Gandhari's curse, because of the Brahmins' curse, and (the final cop-out) it was fated. The word translated here as "fate" is *daivam*, derived from the word for god (*deva*, cognate with *deus*, *theos*) but designating a force that controls the gods as well as humans.

Throughout the text, beginning in the very first book and often repeated elsewhere, it is said that the gods purposely instigated the devastating war to relieve the burden of the earth. The earth, overburdened by evil kings—or, in other versions of the story, by the over-prosperous and hence overpopulating virtuous kings— began to sink beneath the cosmic waters. (A miniature preview of this crisis occurs when the city of Dvaraka is flooded.[94]) To save the earth by lightening her burden, the gods agreed to become incarnate on earth, taking various measures to kill off all the evil (or, as the case may be, virtuous) kings in the great battle. Another variant of this myth tells us that when the gods conquered the demons in heaven, the demons went down to earth, taking human forms, and so the gods, too, took human forms on earth to combat the now human demons. And at the end, when the gods had beaten the

[94] 16.6.8–11, 16.8.40–41.

demons on earth, they went back up to heaven.[95] The argument that all the people who seemed to be tragically killed in the battle were actually incarnate gods who were happy to return at last to heaven is made at some length on several occasions.[96] The discussion of the heroes merging with gods in heaven in the final book essentially rewinds the beginning of the first book of the *Mahabharata*, the *Adi Parvan*, in which the gods become incarnate on earth.

Although everyone keeps telling Dhritarashtra that he was wrong not to restrain his evil son Duryodhana from waging the devastating war, sometimes they say (to console him) that Duryodhana was doing a great and good thing in removing the earth's burden of excess population.[97] Apparently it is an excuse that can be used in many ways. Krishna uses it often. For most of the *Mahabharata*, Krishna is simply a powerful human; he is Arjuna's cousin (since Krishna's father, Vasudeva, was a brother of Kunti, Arjuna's mother) and also Arjuna's brother-in-law (since Arjuna is married to Krishna's sister, Subhadra). But in several passages, notably throughout the final books that concern us here, Krishna is regarded as God. And as God, Krishna is the one who promises to relieve the earth's burden by making sure that there will be a great war in which all the kings and their people will be killed. And so, time and again, the text tells us that Krishna could have intervened to stop the war because he was omnipotent and omniscient, yet, precisely for that reason, he refrained from interfering.[98]

In an interesting twist, Gandhari curses Krishna for failing to stop the war when he could have done so, not because she regards him as an omnipotent deity, but simply because she regards him as a powerful human politician, a spy who knew all the secrets on both sides and could have given them advice that would have prevented

---

[95] Wendy Doniger O'Flaherty, *The Origins of Evil in Hindu Mythology* (Berkeley: University of California Press, 1976), pp. 248–271.
[96] Notably in 15.39 and 18.4–5.
[97] 11.8.20–27.
[98] 16.2.13–14, 16.3.21.

the war.[99] Acting as a human rather than a god, not only does he kill many people himself[100] but he also sends his people out of the safety of the city of Dvaraka on a doomed pilgrimage.[101] Ostensibly a sacred act, a pilgrimage is often a secular event, a breaking away from conventional restraints.[102] The official purpose of the pilgrimage from Dvaraka is to appease the gods and avert the predicted calamity. But, in fact, the pilgrimage gets the men out of the area where liquor is prohibited, which makes it possible for them to get drunk (beyond the bounds of the king's decree of prohibition) and hence precipitates the calamity. Of course, Krishna knows all this. Did he therefore *intend* for the men to get drunk? Krishna's complicity in the holocaust again raises the more general question of the amorality of the gods or, at the very least, their total disregard for the welfare of human beings on earth.[103]

Another reason that the text offers, from time to time, for various deaths is simply "Time." The Sanskrit word *kala* (from the verb *kal*, to count, cognate with the English "calculate") means "time," "death," "fate," and "doomsday"; to signal this range of meanings, I will capitalize the first letter. To "make one's Time" is a Sanskrit way of saying, "to end one's Time," that is, "to die." The word *kala* is also the base of the name of Kali, the spirit of the disastrous Kali Age, the present age. (This Kali is to be distinguished from Kali with a long "a" and a long "i," the name of a great and often destructive black goddess. *Kala* also means "black.")

There are four ages in Indian mythology, waning in quality, like the four ages of Greece, but named not after metals, like the Greek, but after throws of the dice. The first age, the Winning Age, is the throw of four (Krita); the Second Age is the throw of three (Treta); the Third Age is the throw of two (Dvapara); and the

---

[99] 11.25.30–40.
[100] 16.4.35, 44.
[101] 16.3.22.
[102] See Ann Grodzins Gold, *Fruitful Journeys: The Ways of Rajasthani Pilgrims* (Long Grove, IL: Waveland Press, 2000).
[103] Doniger O'Flaherty, *The Origins of Evil*.

last age, a time of disease and disaster, is the Kali Age, the losing throw, snake eyes or craps. The Kali Age began right after the end of the great Bharata war; it is the time in which we live now. (The Kali Age is also said to have become incarnate in the arch villain Duryodhana.[104]) Time is also the explanation for the loss of the first age, the Winning Age: the mere passage of Time made people simply stop being good, and then it was downhill all the way to the Kali Age.[105] This is the world that we are left with after the war in the *Mahabharata*, the world that our protagonists struggle to make sense of in the last books of this great text, the books that concern us here.

The best description I know of the force of the Kali Age in the *Mahabharata* was written by Arshia Sattar:

> This story is about the end of Time as we have known it and lived it. Much of what happens in the *Mahabharata* is predicated on misplaced ambition, greed, envy and lust. And much of this is played out in the most intimate of human relationships— brothers, cousins, friends, wives and husbands, teachers and disciples, elders and the boys that they have trained to be men. Everyone is a rival, everything is contested, hatred and violence simmer under the surface and the skies are dark with suspicion and doubt: Dhritarashtra's literal and metaphorical blindness, Bhishma's moral impotence, Duryodhana's smoldering anger at being ignored and disrespected, Yudhishthira's naive passivity in the face of impending disaster, Bhima's aggression, Arjuna's clinical, single-minded focus on his own glorious destiny, the stifled suffering and sustained humiliation of all the women in the story.[106]

---

[104] 15.39.10.
[105] Doniger O'Flaherty, *The Origins of Evil*, 17–29.
[106] Arshia Sattar, "Writing in Darkness. What It Means to Write and Publish Books on the *Mahabharata* and the *Ramayana* During the Pandemic." *Scroll.in*, November 14, 2020.

Time stands for the inevitable entropy of all things; often when bad things start to happen in the *Mahabharata*, someone simply says, "Time! Time!" The term *kala-paryaya*, literally the turning or twisting of Time, which is often cited as an explanation for an otherwise inexplicable catastrophe, means both that Time is turning back—that a curse from the past has come forward to work its effect now—and that Time has twisted in an evil way, that it has become per-verse (literally, turned wrong). I will call it "the twisting of Time," meaning both that Time twists certain events and that Time itself is twisted by other forces. Time appears personified as a most sinister character along with other bad omens.[107]

In addition to these more general causes of death, particular deaths often result from curses. The basic curse on humankind is universal: everyone dies. Narrowing the field slightly, we know that most of the heroes of this war will die in battle. But the disaster in Book Sixteen, The Battle of the Clubs, is first attributed to the specific curse given by Gandhari and then further narrowed and nuanced, years later, by a curse given by a group of sages to several young boys who are foolish enough to try to play a trick on three of the most famous and formidable sages in ancient Indian mythology. The curses of powerful, and often irascible, sages precipitate much of the action throughout the story.

A curse does not actually make things happen. It is spoken in reaction to an evil act that someone has committed, an act that, by the laws of *karma*, will inevitably cause some great harm to the perpetrator, even if no curse is spoken. But the curse tells the recipient precisely how, and usually when, the retribution will occur. One of the words for a curse, *danda,* literally "rod," means both "curse" and "punishment."[108] The evil act itself sets the ball of karmic retribution in motion; the curse simply puts a spin on it, narrowing down the rut in which the ball runs, from its original

[107] 16.3.1–2.
[108] 16.1.9.

vague headlong flight toward disaster, toward a more specific time and place and agent involved in the disaster. The people who utter the curses are not making anything happen; they are just adding details (and, when the curse is given by a power person, force) to the tragedy already determined by the action of the person who is now cursed, who carries his own curse inside him. The curse serves, moreover, to reveal the plot structures of *karma* to the readers and hearers of the story.

Vengeful Pride as a Cause of War

In the last book, Book Eighteen, it appears at first that the wrong people get to heaven and to hell, and the text goes to some length to explain the rationale for this. But we also discover that even the bad people will be better in heaven. This contradicts the assumption held by most of the people in the *Mahabharata* before their arrival in heaven. For instance, at one point, Gandhari wonders if Shakuni (whose crooked dice game robbed Yudhishthira of his kingdom) will be just as destructive in heaven as he was on earth, assuming both that he will be in heaven and that he will still be evil.[109] She is right on the first guess, wrong on the second. For, as we learn in the final chapters of the *Mahabharata*, even people who have done bad things do often eventually end up in heaven and cease to do bad things, in part because no one in heaven ever seems to do anything at all.

One of the most important ways in which life in heaven differs from life on earth is that, as the gods explain to the newly dead heroes who arrive there, there is no *manyu* in heaven. *Manyu* is an untranslatable word that encompasses the concepts of bravado, pride, hot temper, aristocratic arrogance, aggressive volatility,

[109] 11.24.20–25.

machismo, and balls,[110] all that goes into warrior pride, somewhat like the parallel Greek term *thumos*. (The very word for heroism, in Sanskrit [*vairam*, cognate with the English virility] already also signifies hostility, a grudge, a quarrel, a feud.[111]) The English word "brook," now seldom used, captures a lot of *manyu*: an aristocratic warrior does not "brook" insults. For non-aristocrats, *manyu* says, "I don't take nothing from nobody." More particularly, *manyu* implies that an implied insult must be avenged, and so I have settled for calling it "vengeful pride." The dead warriors, first seen in a vision, then together in heaven at the end of the book, no longer have *manyu*.[112] Heaven is where *manyu* goes to die. But Nilakantha, speaking of Yudhishthira's resentment of his enemies in heaven,[113] says that the predominating power of residual mental impressions (*samskaras*) is expressed by showing that even in heaven, it is hard to give up one's inability to bear the success of enemies. This is a human failing well captured by *manyu* and its negative complement, the German term *Schadenfreude* (rejoicing in someone else's harm).

People in the early books of the *Mahabharata* regard *manyu* as a Good Thing. Draupadi, always ready to berate her husbands for their lack of gumption, initiative, and courage, says to Yudhishthira on one such occasion, "When you see Bhima, who deserves to be happy and is miserable, why does your *manyu* not rise up and grow strong?"[114] Which is to say, "If you have any balls, why don't you *do* something about this?" Draupadi then states outright that no

---

[110] I am grateful to James Kalven for suggesting that "balls" would be an appropriate translation of *manyu* into contemporary American slang (in Chicago on October 7, 2020). Peter Finch in the film *Network* expresses some aspects of *manyu* when he shouts, "I'm mad as hell and I'm not going to take this any more."
[111] The Sanskrit word *amarsha* similarly combines the meanings of envy, resentment, vindictiveness, impatience, anger, and indignation.
[112] 15.40.15, 15.41.6.
[113] In his commentary on 18.1.6.
[114] 3.28.20–29.

warrior in this world (perhaps as opposed to the world of heaven?) can exist without *manyu*.[115]

It is only when the drunken warriors are overcome by *manyu* that they break the rules and set off the chain of events that results in the final slaughter.[116] And only when the incarnate god himself, Krishna, is overcome by *manyu*, does he forget his divine indifference and start killing people.[117] The happy warriors who return on a brief visit from heaven have given up their *manyu*.[118] At the end of his life, reconciled at last with his former enemies, Yudhishthira says that there is no *manyu* left in him.[119] And, finally, only when Indra urges Yudhishthira to give up the *manyu* that is keeping him from sharing heaven with Dhritarashtra and Duryodhana,[120] and only when the former enemies relinquish their *manyu* in heaven, do they find their final peace.[121] To the extent that *manyu* is the essence of masculinity, it would seem that one of the things that the *Mahabharata* heroes must slough off along with the rest of the mortal coil is their very masculinity.

Manyu is what requires a hero to respond to violence with further violence; it is what is responsible for the endless chain of killing. In retrospect, *manyu* turns out to have been at the heart of the problem of devastating human strife, as well as divine anger. That people who have killed one another's sons and fathers and brothers need to give up their *manyu*, to renounce revenge in order to live together in peace in heaven, is this text's answer to a question that continues to plague us to this day, the problem of peace and reconciliation, the problem of ending the chain of retributive violence. In this way, the text produces an extraordinary critique of its own social values—and ours.

---

[115] 3.28.34.
[116] 16.2.9, 16.4.31.
[117] 16.4.21.
[118] 15.40.15, 15.41.6.
[119] 15.44.16.
[120] 18.1.21, 18.3.11.
[121] 18.3.41 +.

INTRODUCTION 39

Part IV: An Apology for My Translation

Criticizing the Critical Edition, and Leaving Key Words in Sanskrit

The editors of the critical edition, working within the limits of their own text-critical goals, often leave out material that makes better sense than the reading they have chosen or that adds something of interest and meaning that the chosen reading lacks. They have, however, very thoughtfully put the rejected material into the critical apparatus, and I have put some of this excised material back into the main text, setting it in italics to indicate that it is material rejected by the critical edition (and identifying, in Appendix 6: Technical Textual Notes, the manuscripts from which each excised/inserted passage is taken).

The last chapter in particular is full of false endings, restarts, more false endings, as if the poets couldn't find the right way to tie it all up, as if they realized that it was impossible to tie it all up. Part of this is the manuscript history; apparently the last books tend to fall more easily off the shelf, or the camel's back, or to be eaten first by the white ants. In any case, there are a number of different, often very interesting, endings rejected by the critical edition, and I have included several of them, again in italics.

Several key Sanskrit words have no simple English equivalent, and I have left them in Sanskrit, as I have left the names of the four ancient Indian classes—Brahmin, Kshatriya, Vaishya, and Shudra. I am also counting on the reader to make the effort to learn four Sanskrit words—*karma*, dharma, yoga, and *tapas*. The first three have already taken on new, often misleading, lives in English (*faux amis*), and I have already used, and briefly defined, all four of them in this introduction. *Karma* (as well as *kala*, Time) I have discussed at some length. That leaves dharma, yoga, and *tapas* to explain more fully here.

Dharma has many meanings, including the law, the moral law, justice, righteousness, the way things are, the way things are not but should be, and, finally, an important god, Dharma, the incarnation of dharma. I will leave "dharma" untranslated in its noun form and will use "dharmic" to translate all its adjectival forms (*dharmya, dharmatman, paramadharmika*, etc.) to convey the pervasive force of this word in the *Mahabharata*.

Yoga in ancient India is mental concentration. It has nothing at all to do with positions of the body, let alone a way of making your abs stronger and more beautiful. Cognate with the English word "yoke," it designates the harnessing of mental powers in order to control both the mind and the physical body.

Tapas is not Spanish food. Nor is it "asceticism," as it is often translated, implying going without food and/or sex. It is a kind of heat, the product of physical and spiritual praxis aimed at harnessing (yoga again) the mental and sensual faculties in order to trap inside the body the heat that is normally expelled through the indulgence of these faculties. As a result, the person who generates *tapas* gains magical powers, particularly the ability to use the suppressed heat of the body in a number of useful ways, including burning an enemy to death or, on the other hand, begetting a child. I have translated the noun/adjective *tapasvin*, "one who has *tapas*," as "man of *tapas*" (or "woman of *tapas*") or "hermit" or "sage," rather rough English equivalents but a better approximation than the usual translation, "ascetic."

The Sanskrit word *ashrama*, hermitage, is now so well known in English as "ashram" that I have used it in that form.

There are also several other important words that I have translated into English but that need a bit of further explanation.

I have translated *deva* as "god," and *asura* as "antigod," but I have left untranslated the names of a number of supernatural creatures: Apsaras, Rakshasa, Guhyaka, and so forth. They are glossed in Appendix 3: Minor Characters and Classes of Beings.

Gati, literally "going" (cognate with our "go"), designates a destination, particularly a final destination, and most particularly a final rebirth destination. It might be any rebirth, or heaven, or final freedom from rebirth, *moksha*. I will call it a "final destination."

Antahpuram, literally, "inner citadel," which I translate as "the inner quarters," is the part of a palace where women, children, and old people are kept safe, often misleadingly translated as "harem."

"Father" and "mother" are easily translated (from *pitri* and *matri*, Indo-European cognates with English), but they are rather misleading, as they often denote not only the two specific biological parents but also any close older relative, more like "uncle" in Shakespeare or "little mother" in Russian novels. The Pandavas, in particular (whose actual father, Pandu, is dead by the time our portion of the story begins), often address Dhritarashtra and Gandhari as their parents, though they are actually their uncle and aunt. Similarly, *shvashura*, literally "father-in-law," more generally designates any older male relative: Kunti, Pandu's widow, sometimes calls Dhritarashtra (her brother-in-law) father-in-law. He calls her his *snusha*, often translated as "daughter-in-law" but actually designates any young female relative. (He also calls her his *vadhu*, a word that can mean "wife" or, again, any female relative.) These usages (traces of which remain today in Hindu joint families, where, for example, most older males are called father-in-law) can be misleading until you get used to them. Often, for the sake of clarity, I omitted the term or added or substituted either an all-purpose relationship or the person's proper name.

The Problem of Adjectives and Epithets

As I worked through the translation, I began to feel that my English text was weighed down and blurred by the repetition of certain words and phrases that had in Sanskrit only a formulaic function that was lost in English. For example, it is a convention of Sanskrit, particularly in this text where so much of the story is told through conversations, to indicate the shift of speakers by the Sanskrit phrase "*ityuktas*," meaning, "when he had been addressed in this way." Had ancient Sanskrit had the use of a close-quotation mark, the poets might have used that instead. To avoid peppering the translation with "he said, he said," I have generally left out the "*ityuktas*." In this I am supported by Francis Cornford, the translator of the Platonic dialogues, who encountered a roughly similar problem:

> Much more space has been saved by leaving out many of the formal expressions of assent interjected by Glaucon and Adeimantus, and thus allowing Socrates to advance one step in his argument in a single connected speech . . . . The convention of question and answer becomes formal and frequently tedious.[122]

What's true of Plato, I think, is also true of Vyasa.

But other recurrent verbal conventions posed other sorts of problems. Many words, primarily laudatory adjectives, epithets, and vocatives that are not unique to a particular person, are used so promiscuously that they no longer carry particular meaning in specific verses. Just as in Lake Wobegon all the children were above average,[123] in the *Mahabharata* every man is wise, noble; every warrior is a hero, a bull among men; every king is a destroyer of his enemies, a protector of dharma; and every woman is beautiful, virtuous, narrow-waisted, and devoted to her husband. These stock adjectives of flattery soon ring hollow.

---

[122] Francis Madonald Cornford, *The Republic of Plato* (New York: Oxford University Press, 1941), vii. Thanks to David Tracy for this reference.

[123] Lake Wobegon was the mythical town which Garrison Keillor created as the setting of the "News from Lake Wobegon" segment of the radio program *A Prairie Home Companion*.

The epithets of the main characters pose additional problems. Many epithets are specific to a certain person, either the person's name or patronymic or matronymic, or a flattering description of a unique physical characteristic or a reference to his past accomplishments. When clustered together, as they often are, they read like a CV or a Wikipedia entry. Even in isolation, such epithets in English sound archaic and give the text an orientalist flavor, like the Shakespearean conventions that the players in *Beyond the Fringe* satirized, bandying about phrases like "our sweetest Essex," "brutish Bolingbroke," "bold Dorset," "bold York," "sweet Norfolk," "faithful Chichester," and, best of all, "saucy Worcester."[124] And since several of the main characters also have many epithets unique to them, when any of the more complex or obscure of these epithets appears alone, in place of the character's usual name, the reader may not know at first what character is being referenced. Moreover, several different epithets in a single paragraph may refer to the same character, making it appear, wrongly, that several different people are involved. A particular problem arises with respect to the epithet "Pandu's son," which is applied indiscriminately, and often confusingly, to all five of the Pandavas (while "Kunti's son" is also applied to the three oldest brothers). The problem of epithets is exacerbated when they are used as vocatives. Often there are so many vocatives, both at the start of a conversation and littered throughout, that the speakers begin to sound like salesmen or the sorts of earnest Americans who keep interjecting your name into the conversation over and over again, simultaneously grabbing or poking you, to make sure that they have your attention.

I was tempted to omit the multiple adjectives and epithets and vocatives from my translation to make the English version of the text flow more smoothly, more clearly, and to make more vivid the

---

[124] "So That's the Way You Like It," Peter Cook, Alan Bennett, Jonathan Miller, Dudley Moore, *Beyond the Fringe*, 1962. Thanks to Robbie Ellis and Carl Grapentine of WFMT, emails of July 8, 2020.

relatively few actually meaningful adjectives and epithets that suggest what the character is doing or feeling *at that moment*. I tried this in an early draft, but the result was a curiously stark and colorless text, the *Mahabharata* as written by Ernest Hemingway rather than, say, Sir Thomas Mallory.

The effect of cutting out all the "meaningless" adjectives and epithets reminded me of the time in the nineteenth century when a particular sect of pious Hindus, corrupted by their admiration for Christian monotheism, translated the names of all the different Vedic gods as "God." We can also learn from an old Jewish joke something about the danger of stripping down the language too close to its bare bones. It seems a man decided to open up a pushcart in the Fulton Fish Market in New York. He needed a sign for his cart and remembered that a friend of his who was a signmaker owed him some money, so he asked the friend to repay him by making him, for free, a sign saying, "Fresh Fish Sold Here." The friend agreed with apparent enthusiasm but then began to argue: "You really don't need to say 'Here,' as the sign will be right there on your cart. Just 'Fresh Fish Sold.' And you don't have to say, 'Sold,' as it's clear that you're not giving the fish away, since you're in the fish market. Just 'Fresh Fish.' And you don't have to say, 'Fresh,' as you would certainly not advertise stale merchandise. Just 'Fish.' And, finally, you don't have to say, 'Fish,' because they can see the fish right there. So you really don't need a sign at all."[125] Oh, reason not the need![126]

The fish-sign joke is a parable of the cult of efficiency, and epics are the antithesis of efficiency; they are made for people with lots of time on their hands or who crave extravagance, excess. The adjectives and epithets in Sanskrit give rhythm and some taste of

---

[125] Another object lesson in the danger of stripping the text down too far is provided by Arnold Schwarzenegger's summary of "Hamlet" in the film *Last Action Hero* (1993), in which, near the start of the play, Schwarzenegger, as Hamlet, says to Claudius: "You killed my fodda. Big mistake." And shoots him.
[126] Shakespeare, *King Lear*, Act 2, Scene 4.

the exalted register, as well as a sense of the human qualities that the culture prized. Although the retired warriors often have martial epithets that still cling to them from the good old days, the adjectives that describe them may reflect the fact that they are now old men: they are usually said to be wise or just or generous, but no longer handsome or physically powerful or fearless. And so, when, from time to time, they are still given their own older, flattering epithets of valor and derring-do, the effect is ironic.

I therefore put back in most of the epithets and adjectives and translated them literally. There were several reasons for this decision, in addition to the Hemingway/Mallory problem. In translating I am striving primarily for accuracy, and the constraints of style often conflict with the constraints of literal equivalence. The old sexist saying that a translation (like a woman) cannot be both beautiful and faithful has much truth in it, if you leave out the parenthesis. A translator does hope to give the reader at least some sense of the feeling of the original language, and the epithets and adjectives do convey some of that feeling. Moreover, as W. J. Johnson has argued, "All epithets do have meanings related to the characters' personalities, and therefore they sometimes provide a key to the interpretation of particular passages."[127]

In the end, I decided that the authors of the *Mahabharata* knew better than I did how to create an ancient Indian epic. And so I left the major characters their individual epithets ("Wolf-belly" for Bhima, "Wealth-winner" for Arjuna, and so forth), translated and capitalized, to distinguish them from adjectives that applied to more than one character ("wise," "great-hearted," etc.), which I did not capitalize. (I listed the recurrent adjectives applied to miscellaneous heroes in Appendix 1: Adjectives Applied to Several Characters, and the more particular epithets in Appendix 2: Names and Epithets of Central Characters.) When I kept an epithet,

---

[127] Johnson, *The Sauptikaparvan of the Mahabharata*, p. 133, also citing Georges Dumezil and Madeleine Biardeau.

I usually also supplied the basic name, though sometimes I counted on my readers to remember the primary epithets of the major characters after a few occurrences (or, if they had forgotten them, to look them up in Appendix 2).

But some of the royal epithets in this text pose another problem. Any form of any of the many interchangeable words for "king" becomes confusing when both King Yudhishthira and King Dhritarashtra are present (as they so often are, until Dhritarashtra's death near the end of Book Fifteen), and the text refers to one or the other, or, often, *both*, as "the king," using any of the many words that denote the ruler. (And, to a lesser extent, when the text refers to both Kunti and Gandhari as "the queen.") Sometimes you get a sentence like, "The king said to the king," with no other identifiers.[128] Confusion reigns, and to deal with such instances, I was briefly tempted to borrow from Dr. Seuss and call Yudhishthira and Dhritarashtra King One and King Two. Eventually I decided to add the proper name of the particular king to the general term "king" whenever there was any ambiguity. And so we have, "King Yudhishthira said to King Dhritarashtra."

The royal vocatives pose special problems. Most of the players in this story of a royal dynasty are, after all, kings. The over-abundance of kings was apparently a perennial problem in ancient India, as we learn from a Buddhist text from perhaps the fourth century CE, which criticizes the city of Vaishali where, it alleges, each of the male inhabitants, regardless of his rank or age, thinks of himself, "I am the king" "I am the king."[129] If you lived in the *Mahabharata* and you met a well-dressed stranger it was probably wise to address him as, "Your majesty."

The kings in the *Mahabharata* often address one another, or are addressed by underlings, either by name or by one of the many

---

[128] 15.44.23.
[129] *Mahavastu*, trans. J. J. Jones, 3 vols., The Sacred Books of the Buddhists (London: Pali Text Society, 1976), vol. 2, p. 436. Cf. also *Lalitavistara,* trans. Rajendralal Mitra (Calcutta: Asiatic Society, 1882).

grandiose synonyms for "your majesty." The royal vocatives often indicate respect or the sort of uneasiness that people do have in addressing people of power. When someone is speaking to a king, or asking a person in power for a favor, or, as is so often the case, both at once—asking a king for a favor—it would be natural to include a vocative or two. The flattering vocatives puff the kings up and inspire them to take action, often the action that the speaker is hoping for. Sometimes the omission of all vocatives is a sign of disrespect, as when the boys in Book Sixteen address the great hermits without any terms of honor,[130] or Indra in Book Seventeen bluntly commands Yudhishthira,[131] and to keep such points vivid, it is necessary to keep other vocatives in places where normal respect is given. These repeated royal vocatives therefore do have meaning. And so, though I sometimes substituted or added the basic name (such as Yudhishthira) for a relatively obscure nickname (Ajatashatru, "Having No Equal Adversary"), I generally left the character-specific royal epithets alone, following the anti-Hemingway principle.

But the poet had dozens and dozens of synonyms for "king" to choose from, such as *rajan* (cognate with the Latin *rex*) or *nripa / naradhipa/nripati* (protector of the people) or *mahipala* (protector of the earth), and so on; see the list in Appendix 1. And he generally chose on the basis of meter rather than meaning. Finding the various paraphrases for *rajan* meaningless and distracting, I translated all the basic terms for a king as "your majesty" in the vocative and as "king" in all other cases, regarding this as less intrusive than the myriad tiny variations on the theme. But I translated literally the more complex royal vocatives and epithets unique to a single royal person.

The royal vocatives are further complicated by the problem of the frame. The *Mahabharata* is narrated by a professional bard,

---

[130] 16.2.6.
[131] 17.3.1.

named Vaisampayana, to a king, named Janamejaya, who wants to know the story of his ancestors (the Pandavas) and who interjects questions from time to time. This translation omits that frame, to keep the story flowing without the interruptions, many of which deal with matters extraneous to the final books. But throughout the narrated text, the narrator, Vaisampayana, constantly addresses the hearer, King Janamejaya, in various ways, including both general terms of royal praise and specific family names. Most of these terms and names, particularly the most general epithet, "descendant of Bharata," apply to both Janamejaya and just about any other male in the whole story, since Bharata is the ultimate ancestor of both Janamejaya and all the Pandavas and Kauravas.[132] And so one never knows whether a "your majesty" or a "descendant of Bharata" refers to the king being addressed on the outer frame, Janamejaya (in which case it should be omitted from this translation, which does not include the frame story), or to one of the kings being addressed in the main story, such as Dhritarashtra or Yudhishthira (in which case I would translate the vocative). I have generally omitted this sort of ambiguous vocative, especially when it contains the element of "Bharata," and more especially when it occurs at the end of a line, where the poet is more likely to be using it just to fill the line.

The Poet and His Formulas, or Parry and Lord to the Rescue

But why would the poet use a vocative just to fill out a line? And why are so many repeated adjectives and epithets scattered through the text, apparently at random? The best answer I know to these questions comes from the works of Milman Parry and Albert

---

[132] As the story is being told to Janamejaya, the text occasionally refers to Parikshit as "your father" (i.e., Janamejaya's father) and to the Pandavas as "your forefathers" (Janamejaya's forefathers). In such cases, I just substitute for those phrases the names of Parikshit and the Pandavas.

Bates Lord. Here, in the service of full disclosure, I must confess that, in my youth, I studied at Harvard with Albert Lord as well as with Milman Parry's son Adam.[133] I was therefore branded at an early age with what came to be known as their theory of Homeric economy.[134] The basic argument is that the Homeric poems were composed and transmitted orally, and that, to help with their improvisation, Homeric poets had a repertoire of set phrases, which included both brief epithets and longer passages, which they could introduce whenever they needed time to think of the next line. Each of the main characters had a number of epithets, each with a different metrical pattern, which the poet applied not according to the appropriateness of the meaning of the phrase but according to its meter, as needed to fill out the metrical pattern of the line in question. (This process is the rough equivalent of what orchestral musicians call "vamping" or "noodling," the repetition of basic chords in the relevant key, which players employ when they've lost their place in the score and just have to keep the rhythm and key going until they can find their place again.) Later studies, one by the great Daniel H. H. Ingalls, have argued that the *Mahabharata*, too, was composed as well as transmitted orally and that similar formulaic strictures operate here.[135] Ruth Katz has argued that Arjuna's

---

[133] Adam Parry taught me some Greek during his brief stint of teaching at Harvard, before he died in a motorcycle accident at the age of forty-three in 1971. His father, Milman Parry, had died of apparently accidental gun wounds at the age of thirty-three. The *Mahabharata* does not have a copyright on doomed scholars. See Wendy Doniger, "How to Escape the Curse," review of John Smith, *The Mahabharata*, for the *London Review of Books*, October 8, 2009.

[134] The theory is perhaps best known through Lord's books, *The Singer of Tales* (Cambridge, MA: Harvard University Press, 1960) and *Epic Singers and Oral Tradition* (Ithaca, NY: Cornell University Press, 1991). See also Milman Parry, *The Making of Homeric Verse: The Collected Papers of Milman Parry*, ed. Adam Parry (Oxford: Oxford University Press, 1971).

[135] Daniel H. H. Ingalls and Daniel H. H. Ingalls, Jr., "The *Mahābhārata*: Stylistic Study, Computer Analysis and Concordance," in *Essays on the Mahābhārata*, ed. Arvind Sharma (Leiden: Brill, 1991), pp. 19–56. Ingalls, who was my *Doktorvater*, was a close friend of Albert Lord. Nabaneeta Dev Sen, too, wrote on the formulaic structure of the *Ramayana* in her M.A. thesis in comparative literature at Harvard University, in 1961, working with Ingalls and Lord, but she never published it.

epithets are formulas used to fill out the meter in lines of verse, rather than to convey a meaning appropriate for that particular context.[136] But many of the major text critics of the *Mahabharata* insist that the epic was composed in writing from the start. At best, some grant that at least parts or aspects of the text may have been composed orally.[137]

I am, I must confess, still a Parry-Lord disciple, and my view is that the early composition of the Homeric epics was oral, though the final recension we have was probably the work of a poet, or, more probably, two poets, one for each of the two Greek epics. We know that the *Mahabharata*, too, has been transmitted both orally and in manuscripts for many centuries. And so I think at least one purpose of the recurrent epithets and adjectives in the *Mahabharata* may have been to allow the bard, whether composing or retelling, to catch his breath.

The Sanskrit poet has his palette of long and short syllables to arrange in the rather simple rhythm of the *shloka* (the verse form in which the *Mahabharata* is largely composed), with no rhyme and no constraints as to word order,[138] the Sanskrit equivalent of blank verse. Whenever the poet got into trouble with a line, he could put in the lifesaving epithet right there and then just go on as if nothing had happened. The "your majesties" that pepper the text also probably serve this purpose. The completely random distribution of the "your majesties" addressed to Janamejaya in the contextless frame, is further support for the argument that these phrases are there only to fill out the line.

---

[136] Ruth Cecily Katz, *Arjuna in the Mahabharata: Where Krishna Is, There Is Victory* (Columbia, South Carolina: University of South Carolina Press, 1989), p. 277.

[137] See the critique of Sukthankar by Alf Hiltebeitel, *Rethinking the Mahabharata. A Reader's Guide to the Education of the Dharma King* (Chicago: University of Chicago Press, 2001), pp. 105–106.

[138] The lexicographer Monier-Williams defines the *shloka* as follows: "a kind of common epic metre (also called Anushtubh) consisting of 4 *padas* or quarter verses of 8 syllables each, or 2 lines of 16 syllables each, each line allowing great liberty; . . . but the 6th and 7th syllables should be long; or if the 6th is short the 7th should be short also."

But just as significant as the question of possible conditions of creation are the conditions of transmission. The bard singing the poem wants to string out the recitation as long as possible. (We get an idea of what the ancient bard could do when he was let loose on an audience, in the over-the-top descriptions that Sanjaya indulges in when asked to introduce the Pandavas, and more particularly their royal wives, to a group of hermits who surely had no idea what he was talking about).[139] The audience, too, would like to make the performance last as long as possible; they can also use the repetitions like a guard rail, to steady themselves through the twists and turns of the story. The repetitions, in Sanskrit, also contribute to the beauty of the poetry, the hypnotic rhythm, and the ritual pleasure, like the pleasure of reciting a poem that everyone knows well. This is true even, or especially, of what George Orwell called "good bad poetry," like a lot of Kipling's,[140] or the reassuring structure of a ballad or a hymn, in which the same refrain is repeated over and over. We know this pleasure from Handel operas in which the whole verse of an aria is repeated several times: if you liked it once, you'll like it again and again. The repetitions also make it easier for the audience as well as the poet to memorize large swaths of material.

But since we encounter these epics as individual readers rather than groups of listeners, we become impatient with all the repetitions that we would never complain about in a ballad. The musical charm of the epithets in Sanskrit is lost in English, where they sound stilted. What is enjoyable in a group—and in a performance and in the original language—is not so much fun when you're reading it alone in an English translation. Considerations such as these also plagued Cornford in his translation of the Platonic dialogues:

---

[139] 15.32.
[140] George Orwell, "Rudyard Kipling" (review of T. S. Eliot's *A Choice of Kipling's Verse*), in George Orwell, *A Collection of Essays* (Garden City, NY: Doubleday, 1954), 116–131.

Some authors can be translated almost word for word. The reader may fairly claim to be told why this method cannot do justice to the matter and the manner of Plato's discourse. In brief, the answer is that in many places the effect in English is misleading or tedious, or grotesque and silly, or pompous and verbose. Since no scholar would apply most of these epithets to the original, there must be something wrong with the current practice of translators.[141]

Alas, I fear that Cornford is right about both Plato and the *Mahabharata*. There is always something wrong with any "current practice of translators." The attempt to accommodate Sanskrit epithets and adjectives in English is just one part of what is inevitably a highly subjective process, that begins every time the translator chooses which English word to use, out of often as many as a dozen English words, to render one Sanskrit word that has many quite different meanings. That is why there are so many translations of great works, all flawed in one way or another. This is my translation of the last books of the *Mahabharata*.

---

[141] Cornford, *The Republic of Plato*, p. v. He goes after Jowett in particular.

THE TRANSLATION

Book Fifteen, *Ashramavasika Parvan*, The Book of Living in the Ashram
Chapters 26–47

Preface to Book Fifteen

Book Fifteen is divided into three sub-books or parts of disparate lengths, each of which is divided into chapters:[1] *"Part One: Living in the Ashram" [Ashrama-vasa], Chapters 1–35; "Part Two: The Vision of the Sons" [Putra-darshana], Chapters 36–44; and "Part Three: The Arrival of Narada" [Narada-gamana], Chapters 45–47. Each of the three passages translated here (the second half of Part One, and all of Parts Two and Three) begins with the arrival of Narada. Part Two doubles back to begin again precisely where the second half of Part One began (Chapter 26).*

The first 25 chapters of Part One consist largely of arguments between the blind King Dhritarashtra, who is determined to retire to the forest, and the five Pandavas, sons of Dhritarashtra's dead half-brother Pandu, who try in vain to persuade Dhritarashtra to remain with them in the royal city of Hastinapur. My translation takes up the story in the last 10 chapters of Part One and continues through all of Parts Two and Three.

We pick up the story when Dhritarashtra has gone to live in the forest ashram of Shatayupa, a royal sage who handed his kingdom over to his son in order to retire to the forest. With Dhritarashtra in

---

[1] Sanskrit calls both the parts and their constituent chapters *parvans*.

56   THE LAST BOOKS OF THE *MAHABHARATA*

the forest are his wife Gandhari, who wears a blindfold in sympathy with her blind husband, and Pandu's widow Kunti. (Madri, Pandu's other wife, had died on his funeral pyre.)

They are attended by Vidura, the half-brother of Pandu and Dhritarashtra, and Sanjaya, Dhritarashtra's charioteer and bard. Later they will be visited by the next generation, whom they had left behind in Hastinapur, a large entourage including the five Pandavas (Yudhishthira, Bhima, Arjuna, and the Twins, Nakula and Sahadeva), their shared wife Draupadi, and Arjuna's wife Subhadra. But now, they have other visitors.

Part One: Living in the Ashram

Chapter 26: Narada Arrives and Predicts Dhritarashtra's Arrival in Heaven

[1–5] A group of distinguished sages came to see King Dhritarashtra: Narada, Parvata, and Devala, great in his *tapas*, and Vyasa of the Island, with his students, and other wise perfected beings, and the old and most dharmic royal sage Shatayupa.[2] Kunti paid homage to the sages with the proper ceremony and gratified them by her service. There the great sages talked together about dharma, to the delight of great-hearted King Dhritarashtra. In the course of one of these narratives, the divine sage Narada told this story of events that he had seen with his own eyes:

[6–13] "Once upon a time, there was a king named Sahasrachitya, the grandfather of Shatayupa. He was the equal of the Creator and feared nothing. Establishing his most dharmic eldest son in the kingship, the dharmic King Sahasrachitya entered the forest. There

---

[2] Though the ashram is Shatayupa's, he joins the visiting sages when they go to see Dhritarashtra.

the high-minded king reached the far shore of his blazing *tapas* and entered the home of Indra,[3] the Shatterer of Citadels. I had chanced to see the king before on many occasions, your majesty, and now that his faults had been burnt away by his *tapas*, he was in Great Indra's palace. So, too, King Shailalaya, the grandfather of Bhagadatta, had reached Great Indra's palace by the power of his *tapas*. And then there was King Prishadhra, the equal of Indra Who Bears the Thunderbolt; he too reached the vault of heaven from here by means of his *tapas*. And Mandhatri's son, King Purukutsa, had achieved great success in this wilderness, your majesty. Amassing *tapas* in this wilderness, this king went to heaven, and his wife became the supreme river Narmada. And a most dharmic king named Shashaloman also engaged in *tapas* in this forest and gained heaven.

[14–20] "And by the favor of Vyasa of the Island, you too, your majesty, have reached this *tapas* forest and will achieve the supreme success that is so hard to get. At the end of your *tapas*, tiger among kings, you too, mantled in glory, will go with Gandhari to the final destination of those great-hearted men. Pandu remembers you constantly, your majesty, in the presence of Indra the Slayer of Bala; he will always do what is best for you. And then, because of her willing service to you and Gandhari, the splendid Kunti, your sister-in-law, will go to the same world as her husband Pandu. For Kunti is the mother of Yudhishthira, who is the eternal Dharma. We foresee this with a divine gaze, your majesty: Vidura will enter the great-hearted Yudhishthira,[4] and Sanjaya, purified by his solicitude for you, will enter heaven."[5]

[21–22] The great-hearted Dhritarashtra, King of the Kauravas, with his wife, accepted these words with pleasure. Wisely praising what Narada had said, he gave him special honor. And then all the

---

[3] Indra, king of the gods, rules in heaven.
[4] In 15.33.
[5] Sanjaya's death is never actually narrated, though after the deaths of Dhritarashtra and Gandhari he sets out for the Himalaya, never to return (15.35.33).

assembled Brahmins greatly honored Narada, rejoicing again and again in the pleasure of King Dhritarashtra.

Chapter 27: Narada Predicts Dhritarashtra's Worlds

[1–7] The excellent Brahmins praised what Narada had said, but the royal sage Shatayupa said to Narada, "Well, you, sir, with your great luster, have magnified the Kuru King's faith, and that of all the people, and even mine, too. You are a divine sage whom the world honors. But there is something I want to discuss regarding King Dhritarashtra; listen while I tell you about it. With your divine eye, divine sage, you know the truth about everything that happens. And so you are familiar with men's various final destinations and can see them. You have mentioned the kings who share Great Indra's world, but you have not told us, great sage, about the worlds of this king, Dhritarashtra. I want to hear from you, my lord, what sort of place this king will go to, and when. Tell me the answer to my question." His words went straight to everyone's heart, and Narada, who had great *tapas* and divine sight, replied in the midst of those good men:

[8–14] "I chanced one day to go to Indra's palace, to the powerful Lord of Power,[6] and there, royal sage, I saw King Pandu. And there, your majesty, they talked about King Dhritarashtra and the difficult *tapas* that he had undertaken. There, your majesty, I heard Indra say this: 'King Dhritarashtra, who has an excellent lifespan, has three years left. Then this King Dhritarashtra will go with Gandhari to the palace of Kubera,[7] the King of Kings, who will honor him, and he will have a wonderful time. The eminent son of a sage, whose faults will all have been burnt away by his *tapas*, will wear divine

---

[6] Indra's wife is named Power (Shachi), but he is also himself the master of power.
[7] The god of wealth.

ornaments and travel in a carriage that goes wherever one wants it to go.' This dharmic man that you ask me about will move through the worlds of the gods and Gandharvas and Rakshasas at his own will and pleasure. This is a great secret of the gods, but I have gladly told it to you. For you are rich in sacred knowledge and have burnt away your faults by your *tapas*."

[15–16] This honeyed speech from the divine sage pleased and delighted all of them, and the king, too. And so, when they had engaged Dhritarashtra with their conversations, those wise men who had themselves won a good final destination went away as they wished.

Chapter 28: The Pandavas Worry about Their Mother and Dhritarashtra

[1–7] When Dhritarashtra the Kaurava King had gone to the forest, the Pandavas were overwhelmed by misery and grief, tormented by grieving for their mother. All the people of the city grieved like that for the king, and the Brahmins talked together about the king and asked, "How can the old king live in the forest where there are no people? And how can Gandhari, who had been so fortunate, and Kunti? The royal sage deserves comfort, but there is no comfort in that great forest. What state can he be in, knowing with his eye of wisdom that his sons have been killed? What a hard thing to do Kunti has done, not seeing her sons, giving up royal glory and taking her pleasure in forest life. And the self-possessed Vidura, who loves to serve his brother—what state is he in? And the wise Sanjaya, who has always taken care of his master's daily needs?" The people of the city, even the young boys, oppressed by worry and grief, came to one another here and there and talked together.

[8–16] The Pandavas, entirely caught up in their grief, did not live in the city for long, grieving as they all were for their elderly mother, and in the same way for their elderly father,[8] King Dhritarashtra, whose sons had been killed, and for the once fortunate Gandhari, and for wise Vidura. As they kept thinking about them, they took no pleasure in the kingdom or in women or in the study of the Vedas. They felt great distaste for the world, as they worried about King Dhritarashtra and remembered, again and again, the horrible slaughter of their relatives, and the murder of Abhimanyu, who was only a boy, at the head of the battle, and the death of strong-armed Karna, who never fled from combat. And remembering the slaughter of Draupadi's sons, and of other friends, the men were not very cheerful. And constantly worrying about the Earth whose heroes had been killed, and her jewels lost, they could not fall asleep. The two queens whose sons had been killed, Draupadi and the lovely Subhadra, could not take much pleasure in anything and remained miserable. Only when they saw Parikshit—the son of Virata's daughter Uttama, and the future father of Janamejaya[9]—were the Pandavas able to sustain their life's breaths. *Struck down by a wave of grief, their minds reeling, turning their backs on all desires, abandoning pleasures, they who had crushed the kingdoms of their enemies now remained diligently with the people of the city, day after day.*

Chapter 29: The Pandavas Set Out for the Forest

[1–8] In that way, the Pandavas, tigers among men but also their mother's darlings, kept remembering their mother and became more and more miserable. In the past, they had been constantly

---

[8] He is actually their uncle, but the term "father" is being used in the usual loose Indian way.

[9] Parikshit, Arjuna's grandson—being the posthumous son of Uttara (King Virata's daughter) and Abhimanyu (Arjuna's son)—is the miraculous survivor who carries on the family line of the Pandavas by fathering Janamejaya, the king to whom the story is being told on the outer frame.

devoted to their royal duties, but now they performed none of their royal duties anywhere in the city. As if invaded by grief, they took no delight in anything; even when they were addressed, they never returned anyone's greeting. Hard to attack, deep as the ocean, they seemed to have lost their wits, their minds assailed by grief. They who were the joy of the Kurus kept remembering their mother, wondering, "How could Kunti, now so weak, support that aged couple? And how could King Dhritarashtra, his sons killed, with no one to help him, live alone with his wife in a forest that is the lair of wild beasts? And the once fortunate queen, Gandhari, whose relatives are all dead, how can she follow her old, blind husband in the forest that has no people in it?" As they talked in that way, they were overcome by longing and anxiety, and they conceived the idea of going to see Dhritarashtra.

[9–13] Sahadeva prostrated himself before King Yudhishthira and said, "I rejoice to see that you have set your heart and mind on going! Out of respect for your eminence, your majesty, I couldn't tell you of my own hope of going. But how lucky I will be to see Kunti, an old woman with matted hair, engaged in *tapas*, wounded by sharp blades of grass. When will I see our mother, now exhausted and suffering greatly, she who enjoyed such extraordinary comfort, growing up in palaces and tall mansions? Truly, bull of the Bharatas, the final destinies of mortals are uncertain, when Kunti, a king's daughter, is living so wretchedly in the forest."

[14–17] When Queen Draupadi, the best of women, heard what Sahadeva had said, she applauded the king and praised him and said, "When will I see Queen Kunti, if she is alive? What joy we will have with her if she is alive today, your majesty! Let it be your constant resolution to let your mind delight in dharma, your majesty, and you will do what is best for us today. And know that all your daughters-in-law are standing on their toes in eagerness, your majesty, longing to see Kunti and Gandhari and their father-in-law Dhritarashtra."

[18-24] On hearing this from Queen Draupadi, King Yudhishthira summoned all his generals and said, "Marshall my army, with many chariots and elephants. I will see King Dhritarashtra in his forest home." And King Yudhishthira said to the superintendents of women, "Have all my various carriages made ready, and palanquins by the thousands, and carts and stores and tents, and artisans, and guardians for the treasure, to go to the ashram at the Field of the Kurus. And whoever among the people of the city wishes to see King Dhritarashtra, any number so long as they are well equipped and well guarded, let him come too. Have my cooks and superintendents of the kitchen, and an entire kitchen, with all sorts of cooked and fresh foods, be brought along on carts. Proclaim the expedition for tomorrow, without delay, and also have all sorts of pavilions made along the path today."

[25-26] When the Pandava King had given these commands, the next morning he set out with his brothers, with the women and children in front. For five days the king remained like that outside the city, protecting the people as they gathered together, and then he set out for the forest.

Chapter 30: The Pandavas Enter the Forest with Their Army

[1-6] Then Yudhishthira, the Best of the Bharatas, gave the command to the army, which was guarded by men the equals of the Protectors of the Regions of the World,[10] with Arjuna at their head. And the great joyous cry of "Yoke the wagons! Yoke the wagons!" arose, as the horsemen shouted "Yoke the horses! Yoke the horses!" Some men traveled on the wagons, and some on horses swift as thought, or on chariots like cities ablaze with fire. Others on noble

---

[10] Gods guard the directions or regions of the world, sometimes said to be four (N, S, E, and W), sometimes eight (N, S, E, W, plus NE, NW, SE, and SW).

elephants, and some on camels, and others went on foot, armed with barbed darts and knives shaped like claws. The city people and country people followed Yudhishthira the Kuru King with various sorts of vehicles, hoping to see Dhritarashtra. And Gautama Kripa,[11] the teacher, by the king's command took charge of the army as its general and went ahead to the ashram.

[7–14] Then Yudhishthira, the glorious Kuru King, Joy of the Kurus, went out surrounded by Brahmins and praised by the many bards and panegyrists and heralds, with a pale umbrella held over his head, and with a great army of chariots. Wolf-belly Bhima, of Fearful Deeds, Son of the Wind, went out with elephants the size of mountains, all equipped with weapons and implements at the ready. Nakula and Sahadeva, the twin sons of Madri, their armor on and banners unfurled, went forward at a brisk speed, surrounded by mounted horsemen. And Arjuna, brilliant and powerful, followed King Yudhishthira in his chariot that shone like the sun and was yoked with divine white horses. The bands of women, led by Draupadi and guarded by the superintendent of women, went forward in palanquins, dispensing immeasurable wealth. That Pandava army was resplendent with its many men and elephants and horses, resounding with its flutes and lutes. The Bulls of the Kurus went on by stages, making their camps beside lakes and on the charming banks of rivers.

[15] Dhaumya, the Pandava family priest, and the brilliant Yuyutsu[12] had seen to the fortification of the city, by Yudhishthira's command.

[16–18] Then King Yudhishthira went down into the Field of the Kurus by stages, crossing the supremely purifying Yamuna River, and from afar he saw the ashram of Dhritarashtra and Shatayupa, the wise royal sage. Then all the people rejoiced and quickly entered that forest, filling it with their great shouts.

---

[11] The Brahmin appointed to be the teacher of the sons of Pandu and Dhritarashtra.
[12] Dhritarashtra's only surviving son.

Chapter 31: The Pandavas Meet Kunti, Dhritarashtra, and Gandhari

[1–7] The Pandavas got down and from a distance proceeded on foot to the king's ashram, bowing with respect. Then all the city people and the people who lived in the kingdom, and the wives of the Kuru chiefs, followed on foot. The Pandavas came to Dhritarashtra's ashram, but it was empty; only herds of deer were scattered among the plantain trees that graced it. Then some hermits who had taken various vows were filled with curiosity and came there in a group to see the Pandavas when they arrived. King Yudhishthira, in a flood of tears, asked them, "Our aged father, the pillar of the Kaurava dynasty—where has he gone?" They answered him, "He went to bathe in the Yamuna, to get flowers and a potful of water." So they went on, on foot, following the path that those hermits had pointed out to them, and then they saw them all, not far off.

[8–15] They hastened on, longing to see their father, but Sahadeva outran them, speeding toward Kunti. Weeping and sobbing, the wise man touched his mother's feet, and she looked at her beloved son, her face streaming with tears. Embracing her little son with her arms, raising him up, she told Gandhari that Sahadeva had come.[13] But seeing that King Yudhishthira was right there, and Bhima and Arjuna and Nakula, Kunti hastened to them. She went ahead of Dhritarashtra and Gandhari, the couple whose sons had been killed, pulling them with her, and when the Pandavas saw her, they fell on the ground. High-minded King Dhritarashtra, the wise ruler, recognizing them by their voices and their touch, comforted and encouraged them. Shedding tears, the great-hearted Pandavas drew close to Dhritarashtra and Gandhari, and then to their mother, Kunti, following the proper protocol. The Pandavas regained their composure as their mother consoled them, and they themselves took up the pots of water for everyone.

---

[13] Gandhari, being blindfolded, would not otherwise have known who was there.

THE BOOK OF LIVING IN THE ASHRAM 65

[16–20] Then the wives of those lions among men, and the army men and the people of the city and the countryside, saw King Dhritarashtra. King Yudhishthira announced the people to him by their name and family, and Dhritarashtra acknowledged them in return. Surrounded by them, his eyes blurred with tears of joy, King Dhritarashtra thought he was back at home in Hastinapur, just as in the old days. Draupadi the Dark Lady and the other daughters-in-law greeted the wise King Dhritarashtra reverently, and with Gandhari and Kunti he returned their greetings. Then he returned to the ashram where the perfected beings and wandering singers were staying. Crowded with people eager to see him, it was like the sky crowded with constellations of stars.

Chapter 32: Sanjaya, the Bard, Introduces the Pandavas to the Hermits

[1–4] King Yudhishthira sat down in that ashram with his brothers, tigers among men, their lotus eyes shining, and with the eminent hermits who had come from various places and were eager to see the broad-chested Pandavas, sons of Pandu the Lord of the Kurus. They said, "We wish to know which one here is Yudhishthira, and Bhima and Arjuna and the Twins, and the splendid Draupadi." Then Sanjaya the Bard announced who all the men were, and Draupadi, and all the other wives of the Kurus, naming each one by name:

[5–8] "This man, his body tawny[14] as refined river gold, like a full-grown great lion, with a prominent nose and wide-set, long eyes, and a broad, coppery-red mouth, is Yudhishthira, King of the Kurus. And this man who walks like an elephant in rut, ruddy as pure smelted gold, with wide and broad shoulders and long, thick

---

[14] Some of the men and women in this passage are said to have skin that is tawny or ruddy or golden or likened to blue lotuses. The ruddy or golden glow is a warm shade of brown, while the blue is not azure but the particular sheen that very dark skin often has.

arms, is Wolf-belly Bhima. Look, look at him! And this dark young man standing at his side, holding a great bow, like the leader of a herd of elephants, with shoulders as high as a lion's and a walk that sways like an elephant's, with wide lotus eyes, this is the warrior Arjuna. The two excellent men standing next to Kunti are the Twins, like Vishnu and great Indra, unequalled in beauty or strength or good nature in the entire human world.

[9–14] "This woman with wide eyes like lotus petals, just now entering the prime of her life, with a complexion like a dark blue lotus, like the divinity of the city, as if she were Lakshmi standing here incarnate, is Draupadi the Dark Lady. Beside her, standing in the middle, with a superb golden skin like the goddess Gauri incarnate, a great twice-born lady, is Subhadra, sister of the incomparable Krishna who bears the discus as his weapon. And this woman the color of a garland of full-blown blue lotuses, the sister of a royal general who always used to compete with Krishna, is the chief wife of Wolf-belly Bhima.[15] This woman, golden as a garland of *champaka* flowers, the daughter of Jarasandha the famous king of Magadha, is the wife of Sahadeva, Madri's younger son. And standing here, her body as dark as a blue lotus, with eyes wide as lotuses, unequalled on the surface of the earth, is the wife of Nakula, Madri's older son. This woman, ruddy as burnished gold, is Uttara, King Virata's daughter, the wife of Abhimanyu who was killed in battle by Drona and the others, though they were mounted on chariots and he had no chariot; and their son, Parikshit, is here with her.

[15–18] "These women who now wear white upper garments and their hair parted[16] used to be the wives of kings. They are the daughters-in-law of this old king; and there are more than a hundred of them. They no longer have protectors, for their husbands and sons have been killed. I have described to you, from the top

---

[15] This is probably Baladhara, the sister of Shishupala (who challenged Krishna). She is the mother of Bhima's son, Sarvaga (1.90.84–5).

[16] The commentator says that the fact that their hair is only said to be parted means that it is not ornamented. This indicates that they are no longer married women.

down, all these women whom you have asked about, the wives of kings, women of pure goodness, whose piety has given them right understanding."

King Dhritarashtra, best of the old Kurus, surrounded by the sons of kings, then asked them all about their well-being. And when all the hermits had gone, and when the warriors had also left the circle of the ashram and had unharnessed their chariots and horses and had settled down, and the women and old people and children had been well settled, he made the formal inquiry after well-being.

Chapter 33: Vidura Enters the Body of Yudhishthira

[1–9] Dhritarashtra said, "Strong-armed Yudhishthira, my dear boy, are you well? With all your brothers and the people of the city and the countryside? And those who depend upon you for their livelihood, are they, too, free from illness? And your counselors and the band of your servants and the elders, your majesty? Do you still follow the old ways that the royal sages cultivated? And are you able to give generously, without interruption, out of a full treasury? Do you treat, each in the appropriate way, your enemies and friends and those who straddle the fence? And do you make sure the Brahmins get their land grants properly? Bull of the Bharatas, do you satisfy, by your good nature, enemies, elders, people of the city, servants, and your own people as well? Do you perform sacrifices, your majesty, and make the funeral offerings to your ancestors and their gods? And do you honor guests with food and drink? Do the priests in your territory, as well as the Kshatriyas, and the Vaishyas and the Shudras who are householders, take pleasure in their own duties? Do the women and children and old people neither feel grief nor have to beg? And are the daughters-in-law in your own house honored, bull among men? Does this lineage of royal sages never slacken in its customary glory, your majesty, now that you are king?"

[10–14] Yudhishthira, who knew the rules and was prosperous, replied to this inquiry about his prosperity: "Your majesty, does your *tapas* thrive, though you grow weary? And my mother Kunti here, so eager to serve you, is she free from exhaustion? And will her life in the forest also be rewarded, your majesty? And my older mother here, Queen Gandhari, emaciated from the wind and the road she has traveled and all she has lost, is engaged in terrible *tapas*. Does she not grieve for her heroic sons who were killed fighting for the dharma of Kshatriyas? Or does she not constantly curse us as the ones who brought about this evil? And where is Vidura? We don't see him, your majesty. And is Sanjaya well, and is he steadfast in his *tapas*?"

[15–20] Dhritarashtra replied to King Yudhishthira: "Vidura is quite well, my son, and is engaged in fierce *tapas*. He takes no food, eats nothing but the wind; he is so thin that his veins stand out. Sometimes the priests see him somewhere in this desolate forest." Even while he was saying this, King Yudhishthira saw in the distance an emaciated, naked man with matted hair, a piece of wood in his mouth,[17] his body smeared with dirt and streaked with forest pollen. Turning back toward the ashram, the man who had been known there as the king's attendant, the son of a Kshatriya father and Shudra mother, suddenly saw the people. King Yudhishthira all alone ran after this man as he entered the horrible forest, sometimes seen, sometimes unseen. The king ran toward him with all his strength, calling out, "Vidura! I am the king, your beloved Yudhishthira!"

[21–27] Then, in a lonely, deserted place, deep in the forest, Vidura, the best of wise men, stood leaning on a tree. The intelligent King Yudhishthira recognized that intelligent man only by his general shape, for he was almost entirely wasted away.

---

[17] This was done as a kind of discipline.

Standing in front of Vidura, within his hearing, the king said, "I am Yudhishthira," and the other replied with a gesture of understanding. Vidura, deep in meditation, looked right at the king without blinking, yoking his own gaze to the other's gaze. The wise Vidura entered limbs with limbs, placing breaths in breaths, senses in senses.[18] Using the power of yoga, seeming to blaze with the brilliance of the Dharma King, Vidura entered the king's body. And then the king saw the body of Vidura just standing right there, its eyes fixed, leaning on the tree, emptied of consciousness.

[28–32] The brilliant Dharma King, Pandu's son, realized that his own body was many times more powerful than before, and he remembered[19]—for he knew magic—all his own ancient dharma of yoga as Vyasa had told it to him. The wise Dharma King wanted to perform the death rituals for Vidura, to burn him. But then a voice spoke:[20] "Your majesty! This that used to be known as Vidura should not be burnt, for this corpse here is yours too, and he is the eternal Dharma. Vidura will have the worlds called 'Extensive,' because he achieved the dharma of a man of *tapas*; no one should grieve for him."

[33–37] The Dharma King turned back again and reported all of this back to King Dhritarashtra, Vichitravirya's son. The radiant king was most amazed and delighted to hear this, as were all the people, and Bhima and the others. Then King Dhritarashtra said to Dharma's son Yudhishthira, "Please accept this water and roots and fruits from me, for, your majesty, a man's food is considered his guest's food." Dharma's son replied to King Dhritarashtra, "That is

---

[18] Nilakantha says: Yoking gaze with gaze, breath with breath, concentrating the mind and senses right there, he emptied the breath and other senses from his own body and united them with the other's breath and other senses, and then he abandoned his own body, just as water in a jug is poured out into another jug. By the joining of the breaths there is a joining of the senses and the limbs.

[19] Nilakantha says: He remembered that he and Vidura were born from a single person, Dharma.

[20] Disembodied voices appear throughout Sanskrit literature telling the truth, often giving commands. The voice is never attributed to any particular god; it is as if fate itself were speaking.

so!" and ate the fruits and roots that the king offered, and so did his younger brothers. And when they had eaten the fruits and roots and drunk water, they all made their camp at the foot of the trees and spent the night there.

Chapter 34: Yudhishthira Distributes Gifts and Vyasa Arrives

[1–6] That is how they spent that night, a calm night filled with constellations of stars, in the ashram of those men of good deeds. Here and there, they talked together about dharma and politics,[21] and about various paths and ways of life, with many citations from sacred texts. The Pandavas then slept all around their mother on the ground, eschewing their luxurious beds. Whatever food the high-minded King Dhritarashtra had, that was the food of those warriors, and so they passed the night. When the night was over and they had all performed their morning rituals, Yudhishthira, Kunti's son, made a tour around the ashram with his brothers and with the retinue of the inner quarters, the servants, and the family priest, acting according to their pleasure and their instructions, with Dhritarashtra's permission.

[7–11] Yudhishthira saw there altars ablaze with fires, tended by hermits who had been initiated and had made oblations into the fires, altars in the shape prescribed by the Veda, suitable for bands of hermits, covered with masses of forest flowers and giving off the scent of royal incense. Herds of wild animals wandered about undisturbed here and there, and flocks of birds sang fearlessly. The woods resounded with the cries of blue-necked peacocks and the cooing of gallinules, with the lovely warblings of cuckoos, charming

---

[21] Dharma and *artha* (politics, economics, worldly matters) are two of the aims of human life (*purusharthas*). The Pandavas did not apparently talk about *kama* (pleasure), the third, let alone *moksha* (freedom), sometimes listed as the fourth aim but almost never mentioned in the final books of the *Mahabharata*.

to hear, embellished here and there with the chanting of learned Brahmins, and the forest glittered with masses of fruits and roots.

[12–15] Then King Yudhishthira distributed the things that he had brought there for the hermits: pots, some made of gold and some of the wood of fig trees; antelope skins and woolen saddle cloths, sacrificial ladles, earthenware water jugs and cooking pots and pans; and iron pots and various sorts of plates; whatever one could wish for, and as much of it, and anything else that was desired. When the dharmic king had toured the ashram in this way, handing out all that wealth, he returned.

[16–20] Then he saw the wise King Dhritarashtra sitting with Gandhari undisturbed, now that they had completed the daily rituals. And the dharmic king saw his mother Kunti not far off, standing bent over like a disciple, as always doing her dharma. He bowed to King Dhritarashtra and announced his own name[22] and was given permission to sit down, and he sat down on a pillow. Bhima and the other Pandavas greeted King Dhritarashtra, the Bull of the Kauravas, and embraced his feet and sat down, as the king commanded. Surrounded by them, the Kaurava King looked most splendid, like Brihaspati[23] blazing with his sacred glory, surrounded by the gods.

[21–26] When they were all seated like that, the great sages who lived in the Field of the Kurus assembled, with Shatayupa at their head. Vyasa, too, the brilliant Brahmin honored by all the assemblies of divine sages, came to appear before the king, surrounded by his students. Then Dhritarashtra, the Kaurava King, and Yudhishthira, Kunti's heroic son, and Bhima and the others, all stood up and honored Vyasa. Surrounded by Shatayupa and the others, Vyasa said to King Dhritarashtra, "Please be seated." And Vyasa accepted a new seat that had been made just for him, strewn with sacred *kusha* grass and covered with a black antelope skin. All the eminent and

---

[22] Because Dhritarashtra is blind.
[23] Brihaspati is the chief minister or consigliere of Indra, king of the gods.

powerful Brahmins sat around him on the special grass seats for Brahmins, with the permission of Vyasa of the Island.

Chapter 35: Vyasa Explains Who Vidura Was and Offers to Perform a Miracle

[1–10] When all the great-hearted Pandavas were seated, Satyavati's son Vyasa bowed to the king and said, "Strong-armed Dhritarashtra, is your *tapas* thriving? Does your mind take pleasure in forest-dwelling, your majesty?[24] Is there no grief in your heart and mind, your majesty, caused by the destruction of your sons? Is all your knowledge calm, faultless one? Do you keep your understanding firm as you perform the rituals of the wilderness? Is your wife, Queen Gandhari, not overcome by grief? She has great intelligence and wisdom, understands dharma and politics, and knows the reality of gain and loss—does she not grieve? And Kunti, who is always eager to serve you, your majesty, with no thought of herself, who abandoned her own kingdom, does she take pleasure in serving her elders? And does the king, Dharma's son, rejoice in pleasing you? And Bhima and Arjuna and the Twins, are they, too, comforted? Do you rejoice to see them? Is your mind unsullied? Is your consciousness pure, your majesty, and has understanding arisen in you? For this is the triad of what is best for all creatures, your majesty: truth, absence of hostility, and freedom from malice. Have you no regret about forest-dwelling, your majesty? Do you relish the forest food[25] and the houses of hermits?

[11–15] "I know, your majesty, what happened to the great-hearted Vidura through the fate of the very great-hearted Dharma.

---

[24] These first few questions are strikingly similar to those that Yudhishthira put to Dhritarashtra two chapters earlier (15.33), suggesting that they constitute the generally accepted etiquette to use in addressing a forest hermit. But, in this case, the questions immediately get more personal.

[25] Nilakantha (with a different reading) says, Is the forest food easy to get?

For the great-hearted, most high-minded Dharma, with his great intelligence and his great powers of yoga, became Vidura because of Mandavya's curse.[26] Not Brihaspati among the gods, nor Shukra among the anti-gods,[27] is so gifted with intelligence as that bull among men, Mandavya. Using up the power of the *tapas* that he had amassed for a very long time, the sage Mandavya accused eternal Dharma. And so, some time ago, through the Levirate arrangement with a Brahmin, and through me, and through Mandavya's own power, the very high-minded Vidura was born 'in the field'[28] of Vichitravirya, as his son.

[16–22] "Your brother Vidura, your majesty, is the eternal god of gods, whom the poets know as Dharma through their superior memory and meditation. Eternal, he grows ever greater in truth and self-control and restraint, and non-injury and generosity and *tapas*. Yudhishthira, the Kuru King, was born by the power of Dharma's yoga and is known by the name of Dharma, your majesty, with his wisdom and his extraordinary understanding. Like fire, like wind, like water, like earth, like space—that is how Dharma remains both here and there. He goes everywhere, descendant of Kuru, and pervades everything moving and unmoving; the god of gods, he is seen by the perfected beings that have burnt away their faults. He who is Dharma is Vidura, and he who is Vidura is Pandu's son Yudhishthira. Vidura, who remained like a servant in your power, your majesty, is Pandu's son Yudhishthira. How wonderful that your great-hearted, supremely intelligent brother Vidura used the power of his great yoga to enter his very self, Kunti's son Yudhishthira.

---

[26] Here, and through verse 15, Vyasa refers to a story, told at length earlier in the *Mahabharata*, in which the sage Mandavya, wrongly convicted of a crime he had not committed, and impaled alive, cursed Dharma to be reborn as a lowly servant. See the Introduction.

[27] Brihaspati is the chief minister of the gods, Shukra of the anti-gods; both are very cunning.

[28] The Sanskrit legal texts analogize the Levirate to a farmer's ownership of a crop that another man seeds in his field. Cf. Manu 9.32–40. See the Introduction.

[23–25] "And you, too, will soon secure the best fortune. Know, my little son, that I have come here to cut away all your doubts. I will reveal to you the fruit of my *tapas* in the form of a miracle, a deed that was never before achieved by any of the great sages in the world. What superhuman thing would you like to have from me, your majesty? What would you like to see, to touch, or to hear? Tell me and I will do precisely that."

Part Two: The Vision of the Sons

Chapter 36: Narada Arrives and Dhritarashtra Grieves

In the first five verses of this chapter (omitted here, as this translation always omits the frame story), King Janamejaya, asks the bard, Vaisampayana, questions about what the Pandavas ate in the forest and how long they stayed there. To answer him, the bard goes back ten chapters, to Chapter 26, the point at which we began, with the arrival of the sages. He even acknowledges this backtracking, with the phrase, "As I have said." And a passage in one of the manuscripts, translated here in italics, helpfully reviews what has happened so far. This time, however, Narada is already there, and several other sages appear now for the first time. More important, this time it is clear that Yudhishthira and the Pandavas are also there.

[6–15] With the permission of Dhritarashtra the Kuru King, the Pandavas rested and enjoyed various foods and drinks. *For Yudhishthira had come, with his army and his brothers, to see King Dhritarashtra, who had gone to live in the forest. On the first day, their food was water and fruits and roots, and they slept on the ground.* They spent a month in the forest with their armies and the people of the inner quarters. Then Vyasa came there, as I have said. And then, as they were all seated around Vyasa in King Dhritarashtra's presence, talking together, other sages arrived: Narada, Parvata, and Devala, great in his *tapas*, and Vishvavasu, Tumburu, and Chitrasena. With Dhritarashtra's permission, Yudhishthira, the high-minded Kuru King, honored them, too, in the proper way. When Yudhishthira had paid them homage, they all sat down on the very best seats of honor, strewn with sacrificial grass. And when they were seated there, the high-minded King Dhritarashtra, scion of the Kurus, sat down, surrounded by Pandu's sons. Gandhari, Kunti, Draupadi and Subhadra sat down there with the other women. Then they told stories from the ancient sages about the gods and anti-gods, stories of heaven and the highest dharma. And when the conversation was over, the brilliant Vyasa, who had the eye of knowledge and was finest speaker and the best of those who know all the Vedas, enjoying himself, spoke yet again[29] to Dhritarashtra:

[16–21] "I know, your majesty, what, in your heart and mind, you wish to say, as you burn with grief because of what your son did. And the misery that remains in Gandhari's heart, your majesty, and Kunti's, your majesty, and in Draupadi's heart, and the sharp misery that Subhadra, Krishna's sister, holds on to, because of the killing of her son—I know that too. When I heard that you had arrived here, I came here to dispel your doubts, Joy of the Kauravas.[30] And let these divine Gandharvas[31] and the great sages witness today the power of the *tapas* that I have stored up for so long. So tell me, strong-armed king, what desire of yours shall I fulfill? I am inclined to grant your wish. See the power of my *tapas*!"

[22–25] The king thought for a moment about what the immeasurably intelligent Vyasa had said, and then he began to speak: "How fortunate I am, and how grateful I am! My life has borne fruit

---

[29] A reference to his long formal questions at the end of 15.35.
[30] Nilakantha says that the sage spells out what these doubts might be, such as how one could see right before one's eyes a person who had been burnt to ashes.
[31] I have absolutely no idea why the divine Gandharvas, who are celestial musicians, usually expressly contrasted with mortal Gandharvas, should be here on earth with the mortals, but they are mentioned again, still among mortals, in Chapter 39, so the poet did not refer to them here accidentally.

because you came to me here today with your holy men. And today I also understand that my own final destination that I wished for is here, since I have met with all of you who are so like Brahma, so rich in *tapas*, so faultless. I have been purified just by the sight of you; there is no doubt about this. And I have no fear of the world beyond.

[26–29] "But my heart grieves me as I remember how I was always so eager to help my son, that most weak-minded, slow-witted man, with his extremely wicked machinations, that evil-minded man who slaughtered the Pandavas, though they had done no evil, and who destroyed this earth with its horses and men and elephants. And the great-hearted kings, rulers of various countries, who came to me because of my son, all fell into the power of death. Giving up their sons and wives, dear to their hearts, and their own life's breaths, those heroes went to the house of the king of ghosts.

[30–33] "What, Brahmin, was the final destination of those who were killed in battle for the sake of their friends? And, indeed, of my own sons and grandsons who were killed in the war? My heart and mind burn with sorrow again and again when I think of the slaughter of that great army, and of old Bhishma, Shantanu's son, and Drona, the best of the twice-born, and the whole brilliant family, whom my son, the evil fool who hated his friends, destroyed just because he wanted to be king of the earth. As I, his father, keep remembering all of this, worrying, burning up day and night, overwhelmed by misery and grief, I know no peace and find no comfort."

Chapter 37: Gandhari Tells Vyasa of the Women's Grief

[1–14] When Gandhari heard these various lamentations of Dhritarashtra, the royal sage, her grief was made new again, and so was Kunti's, and Draupadi's, and Subhadra's, and that of all the fine women who were the daughters-in-law of Dhritarashtra the Kaurava. Filled with grief for her sons, Queen Gandhari, who had bound her eyes, stood up and cupped her hands in reverence and said to her father-in-law, Vyasa: "These sixteen years have passed, bull among sages, while this king grieves for his slain sons and finds no peace. Filled with grief for his sons, sighing, this king, Dhritarashtra, spends whole nights without falling asleep. By the power of your *tapas*, great sage, you are able to create all the other worlds, and so surely you can also show the king his sons who have gone to other worlds. And Draupadi the Dark Lady here, this good woman, your most beloved granddaughter-in-law, grieves so much for her sons and relatives who were killed. Krishna's sister, too, the beautiful, soft-spoken Subhadra, tormented by the death of her son Abhimanyu, grieves so much. And the wife of Bhurishravas suffers so much grief for the death of her husband that in her great misery she does not sleep at night. Her father-in-law, the wise Bahlika, scion of the Kurus, was killed in the great battle, and his son Somadatta was killed with him. Your wise son Dhritarashtra never fled in battles, but his hundred sons were killed in the war, and his hundred wives here are overwhelmed with grief for their sons, a grief which grows again and again in King Dhritarashtra and in me, throwing me down with new force each time it begins anew, great sage. What was the final destination of my great-hearted and heroic male relatives, Somadatta and the other warriors? By your favor, lord, this king could be free from grief. Let him end his Time[32] soon, and me too, and Kunti here, your daughter-in-law."

[15–18] As Gandhari spoke, Kunti, her face thin from her vow of fasting, remembered her son whose birth had been hidden, the child of the Sun. The sage Vyasa, dispenser of boons, who could see and hear far, saw that Queen Kunti, the mother of Arjuna the Ambidextrous Archer, was unhappy. Vyasa said to her, "You should say what you want to have done. Tell me, wise woman, what is in

---

[32] A particular use of *kala*, "time/death"; see the Introduction.

your heart and on your mind." Then Kunti, bowing with her head to her father-in-law, told this story from the past that, in shame, she had covered up.

Chapter 38: Kunti Tells Vyasa How She Abandoned Karna

[1–8] Kunti said, "Sir, you are my father-in-law, the deity of my deity, the god beyond my god.[33] Listen to my true story. The Brahmin sage Durvasas, an irascible man of *tapas*, came to ask my father for food as alms, and I satisfied him completely with food and with my purity, knowledge of sacred texts, renunciations, and pure mind, and I never grew angry, even when there were good reasons for anger.[34] Pleased with me, he offered to grant me a boon, and when I said, 'No need,' he replied, 'You have no choice but to accept it.' Fearing his curse, I spoke to the Brahmin yet again, and yet again the Brahmin said to me, 'It must be so. You, my lady with the excellent face, are the future mother of Dharma. Whatever gods you summon will be in your power.' And so saying, the Brahmin vanished. I was amazed by this, but my memory did not fail to retain all the details. So I stood on the roof of the palace and watched the sun rising, remembering the sage's words and longing for the sun. I stood there, not realizing my mistake, because I was just a child.

[9–13] "But then the god of a thousand rays came near me, splitting his body in two, on earth and in the sky. With one part he heated the worlds, and with the second he came to me. As I stood there trembling, he said to me, 'Choose a boon from me.' 'Please go,' I said to him, bowing my head. The Sun with his sharp rays said

---

[33] This was a standard way for a woman to address her father-in-law, who, as the father of her husband, encompassed two levels of deity. Cf. 14.93.50.
[34] The story is told, with slightly different details, at 1.104.4–13, 3.290–292, 5.144, 11.27, and 13.144. See the Introduction.

to me, 'You are not allowed to summon me in vain. I will burn you up and also that Brahmin that gave you your boon.' To protect the sage from the curse, since he had committed no offense, I said, 'May I have a son like you, who are a god.' Then, entering me with his fiery brilliance, and stupefying me, the Sun said, 'You will have a son,' and went back to the sky.

[14–18] "To conceal this event in the inner quarters of my father's palace, I took the little boy, my son Karna who had been born in secret, and threw him into the water. And by the god's favor I became a virgin again, just as the sage had promised me, good Brahmin. I was a fool to neglect my son as soon as he was born. And that still burns me, as you know well—for you are a Brahmin sage. Whether this was wicked or not wicked, I have now revealed it. I hope you, lord, will dispel this fear of mine now. And as you know what is in this king's heart, best of sages, faultless one, let him have that wish on this very day."

[19–23] Vyasa, best of those who know the Veda, replied, "You did well to tell me all of this so very truly. And there is no fault in you, for you were made a virgin again. The gods, who have superhuman dominion,[35] can enter bodies. And the bodies of gods are born in five ways: by imagination, by voice, by sight, by touch, and by sexual friction.[36] For the dharma of humans has no connection with the dharma of the gods. You should understand this, Kunti, and let the fever in your mind vanish. Everything is within bounds[37] for those who have brute power; everything is pure for those who have power. Everything is dharma for those who have power; everything of those who have power is their own."

---

[35] Cf. Durvasas's promise, in this very chapter (15.38.6), that the gods would be in *her* power (*vashe*). But here Vyasa uses other words for power: *aishvarya*, superhuman dominion (in verse 20), and *bala*, brute force (in verse 23), four times.

[36] Nilakantha says this friction (*sangharsha*) is *rati*, sexual pleasure.

[37] Literally, "on the path," *pathya*.

Chapter 39: Vyasa Explains the Incarnation of the Gods as Warriors

[1–5] Vyasa said, "My lady Gandhari, you will see your sons and brothers and friends, and the wives with their husbands, as if they had just arisen from sleep in the night. Kunti will see Karna, and Subhadra will see Abhimanyu; Draupadi will see her five sons, as well as her older male relatives and her brothers. I had already resolved before, in my heart, to do precisely what the king, and you, and Kunti now urge me to do. You should not mourn those greathearted men, because, as all of them, bulls among men, cared most about the Kshatriya dharma, they went to that sort of death. You are blameless. What must be is beyond our powers. It is the work of the gods, all of whom descended to the surface of the earth with portions of their divine nature.[38]

[6–15] "Gandharvas and Apsarases, and Pishachas and Guhyas and Rakshasas, Punyajanas and perfected beings, as well as divine sages, and gods and Danavas and flawless Brahma-sages—they went to their death in the great battle on the Field of the Kurus. The wise king of the Gandharvas became known as Dhritarashtra; he lived in the human world as your husband Dhritarashtra. Know that Indra, the Unfallen, the most distinguished Leader of the Band of Winds, became Pandu; and a portion of Dharma became Vidura, an attendant, the son of a Kshatriya father and a servant woman; and a portion became this King Yudhishthira. Fair lady, know that the Kali Age[39] became Duryodhana, and the Dvapara Age became Shakuni, and know that Duhshasana and his people were Rakshasas. Know that the powerful Bhima, subduer of enemies, came from the host of the Winds; and that Wealth-Winning Arjuna, Kunti's son, is the sage Nara, and Spike-haired Krishna is Narayana; and the Twins are the Ashvins, Yama's sons. And know, lovely lady,

---

[38] See the Introduction and 18.4–5.
[39] See the Introduction.

that the Sun, who heats the worlds, greatest of all sources of heat, when he divided his own body in two[40] became Karna, who was born to cause hostility and rivalry. Abhimanyu, the heir of Arjuna and son of Subhadra, who was killed by six warriors, is Soma, who split himself in two here by means of yoga. Dhrishtadyumna, with Draupadi, was born from Fire, and a portion of Fire is the good Rakshasa Shikhandin. Know that Drona is a part of Brihaspati, and Drona's son Ashvatthaman was born of Shiva. And know that Bhishma, the son of the River Ganges, was born when one of the Vasus became a human being.[41]

[16–18] "In that way, wise woman, lovely woman, these gods became human, and so they have now gone back to heaven, since their work is done.[42] Today I will drive away this misery that has lodged so long in the hearts of all of you because of your fear about the world beyond. Go, please, all of you, to the River Ganges, and there you will see all of the people who were killed on this battleground."

[19–24] When the people heard what Vyasa had said, they went toward the Ganges with a great lion's roar. Dhritarashtra and his ministers went first with the Pandavas, accompanied by the tigers of sages and the assembled Gandharvas. The ocean of people went together to the Ganges in the proper order, and they made their night quarters there according to their pleasure and their comfort. Wise King Dhritarashtra settled for the night in a pleasant place with the Pandavas, attended by his followers, with the women and old men going in front. That day passed for them as if it had been a hundred years, as they waited for the night, longing to see the dead kings. At last the sun set behind the auspicious Western Mountain, and then they performed their ablutions and the night ritual.

---

[40] We've seen the Sun do this in order to remain in the sky while he impregnated Kunti and engendered Karna; now he is said to be not only the father but the incarnation of Karna, again simultaneously remaining in the sky.
[41] The birth of Bhishma is told at 1.92. See also 18.5.9.
[42] The final phrase may also mean, "since their karma was finished."

Chapter 40: The Dead Warriors Appear out of the Ganges

[1–5] When night had fallen, and the people who were assembled there had completed the rituals that they did every evening, they all went together to Vyasa. Dharmic Dhritarashtra, purified and single-minded, sat with the Pandavas and the sages. The women sat with Gandhari, and the people from the city and the country sat according to their ages. Then the great and brilliant sage Vyasa plunged into the holy water of the Ganges and invoked all the peoples, the warriors of the Pandavas and the Kauravas, all of them, and the eminent kings who lived in various lands.[43]

[6–13] Then the sound of a great commotion arose from within the waters, like the sound when the two armies of the Kurus and Pandavas met in the past. And then all the kings and their armies came out of that water by the thousands, with Bhishma and Drona at the front. Virata and Drupada came with their sons and their armies, and Draupadi's sons, and Abhimanyu, and the Rakshasa Ghatotkacha. Then came Karna and Duryodhana, and the great warrior Shakuni, and Duhshasana and all the other great warriors who were Dhritarashtra's sons; and Jarasandha's son Bhagadatta, and Prince Jalasandha, and Bhurishravas, Shala, Shalya, Vrishasena and his younger brother Sushena, Prince Lakshmana, and Dhrishtadyumna's sons; and all of Shikhandin's sons, and Dhrishtaketu and his younger brother; and Achala and Vrishaka, and the Rakshasa Alayudha; and Bahlika and Somadatta and Chekitana. These and many others, too many to mention—they all stood up out of the water with shining bodies.

[14–16] Each man among the assembled princes appeared with his own particular clothing and banner and mount. They all wore divine garments, and they all had shining earrings. They were free

---

[43] Nilakantha here supplies a full page of arguments about the way in which magic can make it appear that one can see the bodies of people who have died.

from enmity and free from egoism, and they had lost their rage and their vengeful pride. The Gandharvas sang to them, and the bards praised them, and troops of Apsarases surrounded them, and they wore divine garlands and garments.

[17–21] Then the sage, Satyavati's son Vyasa, pleased with Dhritarashtra, used the power of his *tapas* to give him divine sight. The splendid Gandhari, too, was given the power of divine knowledge and saw all her sons as well as the others who had been killed in the battle. All the people watched this tremendous, unimaginable marvel in amazement, with unblinking eyes and goosepimples on their bodies. That advancing army, crowded with joyous women and men thrilling with the excitement of a celebration, looked like a colored painting on a cloth. And Dhritarashtra rejoiced to see them all with his divine gaze, given by the sage's favor.

Chapter 41: The Returned Warriors Depart and Their Wives Enter the Ganges

[1–7] Then the best of the Bharatas met one another; their anger and envy were gone, and their moral stains. Keeping to the excellent rule that the Brahmin sage had established, their hearts full of delight, they were like the immortals in the world of the gods. Son united with father and mother, wife with husband, brother with brother, and friend with friend. The Pandavas met joyously with Karna, the great archer, and with Abhimanyu and all of Draupadi's sons. The Pandavas were delighted with Karna, and all the kings came together and made friends. By the sage's favor, they and the other Kshatriyas lost their vengeful pride and cast off their unfriendliness and became friends. In this way, all the tigers among men, the Kurus and the men of other lineages, joined their elders and kinsmen and sons.

[8–11] The kings enjoyed themselves to their hearts' delight. For that one whole night, they were as completely happy as if they had been in heaven. Here there was no grief, no fear, no worry, no regret or dishonor, as the warriors embraced one another. And the women, united with their fathers, brothers, husbands, and sons, felt the highest joy and let go of their misery. The men and their women spent that one night in pleasure and then embraced one another and said goodbye and went back as they had come.

[12–17] Then that bull of sages dismissed those people, and in an instant they vanished right before everyone's eyes. Plunging into the holy Ganges that flows through the three worlds,[44] the great-hearted men went back to their own places with their chariots and banners. Some went to the world of the gods, some to the palace of Brahma, some to the world of Varuna, and some to the world of Kubera. Some of the kings had won the world of Yama; some reached the worlds of the Rakshasas and Pishachas, some the Northern Kurus.[45] All the great-hearted men, with their mounts and their foot-followers, went along with the gods to the diverse final destinations that they had won.

[17–23] When they had all gone, that great, brilliant, and dharmic sage, ever eager to do a favor for the Kurus, stood in the water and spoke to the Kshatriya women whose husbands had been killed: "Whatever outstanding women wish to go to the worlds that their husbands have made should plunge into the waters of the Ganges, quickly, without delay." When those excellent women heard his words, which they believed, they bade farewell to their father-in-law, Dhritarashtra, and entered the water of the Ganges. Freed from their human bodies, all those good women were then united with their husbands. Those virtuous women of good family went into the water in the proper order, were freed, and went to the same world as their husbands. They took on divine forms and were adorned with divine jewelry and divine garlands and garments, just

---

[44] The Ganges flows on earth, where it is known as the Ganges, and in heaven, where it is the Milky Way, as well as in the underworld.
[45] A beautiful land in the far north of India.

as their husbands had been. These women of virtue and goodness, endowed with all the good qualities, were now free from mental darkness and weariness, and each went to her own place.

[24–25] At that time, Vyasa, as fond of dharma as a cow of her calf, and always generous with boons, granted anyone whatever desire he had. And men who heard about that return of the man-gods rejoiced and thrilled with excitement, even when they had gone on to other countries. *And all the descendants of Puru[46] who had seen that supreme marvel lost any notion of fear and any moral stain.*

[26–28] *Whatever man hears about this reunion that they had with their loved ones always wins the things he loves, both here and when he dies. And whatever wise person recites to others this effortless and safe reunion with beloved relatives will win supreme success. Men who have mastered their studies, and mastered the rituals, and have achieved the yoga of the Self, and are firm, when they hear this Part[47] unceasingly, they will achieve the highest final destination.*

[**Chapters 42–43:**] *[42] Now Janamejaya, hearing the story in the frame, asks the bard to explain how King Dhritarashtra could see his dead sons. How could there be a vision of a form of people who had cast aside their bodies? [42.2] The bard replies with a somewhat incoherent explanation of the law of karma: not all karmas are destroyed; bodies are born of that unused karma, and they have forms. [42.4] To the extent that karma is not destroyed, to that extent it takes its own form, while men whose karma has been used up take on other forms. [42.8] A man who has become invisible once again becomes visible. [42.16] One experiences with whatever body the Lord makes; one experiences mental things with the mind and bodily things with*

---

[46] An ancestor of both the Kauravas and the Bharatas.
[47] By "this Part [*parvan*]" the poet seems to be referring to the entire second subparvan of the *Ashramavasika Parvan*, "Part Two: The Vision of the Sons [*Putradarshana*]." The list of benefits that will accrue to the reader, known as the *phala-shruti*, the "fruits of hearing," always comes at the very end of the text in question (as it does at the end of the *Mahabharata*, 18.5.35–45). Evidently Part Two once ended here, before the two chapters in the frame (42 and 43) and the bridge chapter (44).

the body. [42.17]. That is, one's actions do not perish but determine the nature of the reborn body, which therefore continues to exist, and to be visible, as a result of its deeds. Then [43] Janamejaya asks if he might see his own dead father, Parikshit, and Vyasa grants him that vision. Finally Janamejaya asks the bard to continue with the story of Dhritarashtra and Yudhishthira.

Chapter 44: The Pandavas Take Leave of Dhritarashtra, Gandhari, and Kunti

[2–4] When King Dhritarashtra, the royal sage, had seen that great marvel, seeing his sons and grandsons and followers again, his grief vanished, and he went back to his ashram. With Dhritarashtra's permission, the great sages and the rest of the people went away as they wished. And the great-hearted Pandavas, with a much-reduced number of soldiers, followed great-hearted King Dhritarashtra and his wife.

[5–9] When Dhritarashtra reached the ashram, Satyavati's son Vyasa, the wise Brahmin sage honored by all the people, said to him, "Listen, strong-armed Dhritarashtra, Joy of the Kauravas. You have heard all sorts of stories told by ancient sages who have grown old in their knowledge and have done good deeds, who are eminent in wealth and high birth, who know the Vedas and their branches and know dharma. Don't set your heart on grief. The wise man has the serenity to accept what he cannot change. From Narada, who has seen the gods, you have heard the secret of the gods. By following their dharma as Kshatriyas, your sons have gone to the auspicious final destination that is purified by weapons; they enjoy doing whatever they like, just as you saw.

[10–12] "But the wise Yudhishthira here, with his brothers and his wife and friends, is entreating you. Let him leave; let him go back and rule his own kingdom. For they have spent a month and more living in the forest. And this land, your majesty, must be constantly and energetically guarded; many people work against the interests of this kingdom."

[13–22] When he heard this from Vyasa, whose intelligence was immeasurable, the eloquent Kaurava King Dhritarashtra summoned Yudhishthira and said, "Yudhishthira, please listen to me, with your brothers. Through your favor, your majesty, grief no longer torments us. I delight in you, my learned son,[48] just as I did before in Hastinapur. As my protector, you follow me and hover closely over those who are dear to me. From you I have gained the fruit of having a son; I take great joy in you. There is no vengeful pride left in me. But you must go, right away, my strong-armed son. For my awareness of you here erodes my *tapas*. And now that I have seen you, my body is again engaged in yoking its *tapas*. Your two mothers here are just like that too; they have eaten nothing but fallen leaves, keeping the same vow that I keep, my son. They will not go on living for long. Through the power of Vyasa's *tapas*, and because of your arrival here, I have seen Duryodhana and the others even though they had gone to another world. The purpose of my long life has been achieved, and now you, my faultless son, should give me your consent to engage in fierce *tapas*. Today, the funeral offerings to our ancestors, and their fame, and the family lineage all depend upon you. My strong-armed son, you must go tomorrow or today, without delay. You have heard a great deal about the science of kingship; I don't see what more is to be taught beyond what has already been done."

[23–26] King Yudhisthira replied to King Dhritarashtra: "You who know dharma should not reject me when I have done nothing wrong. Let all my brothers and followers go if they wish, but I will follow you[49] and my two mothers who are constrained by their strict vows." Gandhari said to Yudhishthira, "You should not talk

---

[48] Throughout this passage, as usual, Dhritarashtra and Yudhishthira address one another as father and son, though they are actually uncle and nephew.
[49] Nilakantha says he means "I will serve you."

like that, my son. Listen to me. The family of the Kurus depends on you, as do the funeral offerings for my brother-in-law.[50] Go, my son. You have done enough, and we are honored. You must do what the king has said, my son, and heed your father's words."

[27–29] Yudhishthira wiped the tears of love from his eyes and said to Kunti, who was also weeping, "The king is sending me away, and so is splendid Gandhari. But how will I bear the pain of leaving? For my thoughts are ever bound to you. Yet I could not bear to pose an obstacle to your *tapas*, as you always act with dharma. For there is nothing higher than *tapas*, and it is through *tapas* that one finds what is great.

[30–35] "Nor do I have the same opinion of kingship, my queen, that I used to have. My mind, with my whole soul, is now devoted to *tapas* alone. This whole earth is empty and gives me no pleasure, fair lady. Our relatives have been decimated, and our power is not what it used to be. The Panchalas have been entirely wiped out, with nothing left but girls. Fair lady, I don't see anyone who could restore their family. For Drona all by himself reduced all of them to ashes in the battle, and in the night Drona's son Ashvatthaman killed all who were left.[51] And so it is with the Chedis and the Matsyas whom we used to see. Only when I see the circle of the Vrishnis, from the household of Vasudeva's son Krishna, do I want to stay, for the sake of dharma, and no other reason. Look on us all with kindness. It will be hard to get to see you, mother, since King Dhritarashtra is going to undertake fierce *tapas*."

[36–41] When strong-armed Sahadeva, commander of fighters, heard this, his eyes filled with tears, and he said to Yudhishthira, "I cannot bear to leave our mother, your majesty. You, sir, should go back immediately; but I will engage in *tapas* in the forest. I will dry up my body with *tapas* right here, as I am committed to serving at

---

[50] This would be Pandu, for whom Yudhishthira, his son, would be the one to offer the yearly funeral sacrifices.
[51] This was the gruesome and shameful night raid, described in Book Ten.

the feet of the king and our two mothers." Then Kunti embraced him, her strong-armed son, and said, "Go, my son, and do not talk like that. Do what I say. Farewell, my little sons, and may your arrivals be auspicious. You would certainly be an obstacle to our *tapas*. Bound by the bonds of my love for you, I would lose my supreme *tapas*. And so, my little son, you must go. For there is little left of us."

[42–47] All sorts of words like that from Kunti stiffened the resolve of Sahadeva and, particularly, King Yudhishthira. And so the bulls of the Kurus took leave of their mother and King Dhritarashtra. They bowed to him, the Best of the Kurus, and began to bid him farewell: "We will go back now, your majesty, gladdened by your blessing. As you have given us permission to leave, your majesty, we will go without offense." The royal sage gave Yudhishthira permission to leave, blessing the great-hearted Dharma King with wishes for victory. And King Dhritarashtra conciliated the mighty Bhima, the best of the powerful, who accepted his greeting in the right spirit.[52] Embracing Arjuna and the Twins, bulls among men, Dhritarashtra the Heir of Kuru gave them leave to depart, hugging and blessing them.

[48–52] They honored Gandhari by putting dust from her feet on their heads, and she gave them permission to leave. Their mother, Kunti, smelled their heads and embraced them, and then they circled her to the right, like calves held back from the cow.[53] Glancing at her again and again, they moved forward, keeping her on their right. In the very same way, good Draupadi and the Kaurava women behaved correctly toward their father-in-law and then went

---

[52] This resolves a very old feud. Bhima had killed Dhritarashtra's son Duryodhana, crushing his thigh and drinking his blood. And later, Bhima had accused Gandhari of being at fault in not restraining Duryodhana (11.14). Even in earlier sections of this Book (15.1, .4, .17–18), there are serious tensions between Bhima and Dhritarashtra: Bhima continues to blame Dhritarashtra for his foolishness, to act against him behind his back, and to refuse to contribute to the funds for the burial of Dhritarashtra's sons. So there is a clear need for reconciliation now.

[53] Nilakantha says, "in order to prevent them from drinking from the udder."

away. Their two mothers-in-law, Kunti and Gandhari, embraced them, blessed them, gave them detailed advice on what it was proper for them to do, and granted them leave to depart, and so they left with their husbands. Then a great roar rang out from the charioteers shouting, "Yoke up!" and from the camels bellowing and the horses whinnying. And then King Yudhishthira, with his wife and his army and his relatives, went back to the city of Hastinapur.

Part Three: The Arrival of Narada

Each of the three parts of Book Fifteen begins with the arrival of Narada, though only this third part is officially given that title.

Chapter 45: Narada Arrives and Tells Yudhishthira How Dhritarashtra, Gandhari, and Kunti Died

[1–4] When the Pandavas had spent two years there,[54] the divine sage Narada chanced to come to Yudhishthira. Strong-armed Yudhishthira, the Kuru King, the best of speakers, honored him, seated him comfortably, and said to him, "It's been quite a long time since I've seen you at my side, good sir. I hope you are in good health, good Brahmin, and are waiting on me for a happy reason. What places have you visited? And what can I do for you? Tell me this, best of the twice-born, for you are our beloved guest."

[5] Narada said, "It's been a long time since I've seen you, your majesty. I've come from my *tapas* forest, after visiting shrines and the Ganges, your majesty."

[6–8] Yudhishthira said, "My men who live on the banks of the Ganges are saying that the great-hearted Dhritarashtra is now

---

[54] In Hastinapur.

engaged in the ultimate *tapas*. Have you seen him there? Is the Scion of the Kurus well? And Gandhari, and Kunti, and Sanjaya the Bard's son? How is my father the king now? I wish to hear if you, sir, have seen the king."

[9–17] Narada said, "Take courage, your majesty, and hear, just as it happened, all that I heard and saw in that *tapas* forest. When all of you had turned back from the life of forest-dwellers, Joy of the Kurus, your wise father went from the Field of the Kurus to Gangadvara[55] with his wife Gandhari, and Kunti, and Sanjaya the Bard, taking with them the materials for the fire oblation and the sacrifice. Your father, so rich in *tapas*, engaged in severe *tapas*, placing a stick of wood in his mouth and living as a hermit, eating nothing but wind. All the hermits in the woods venerated him as one whose *tapas* was great, until, after six months, the king had become nothing but skin and bones. Gandhari, too, lived on nothing but water, and Kunti fasted for a month. Sanjaya fasted "by sixes."[56] They performed the fire sacrifices and offered the oblations according to the ritual rules, both when the king was seen in that forest and when he was not seen. Then the king became houseless and wandered in the forest, and the two queens together followed him with Sanjaya. Sanjaya led the king in the rough places and the smooth, and the blameless Kunti was Gandhari's eyes, your majesty.

[18–21] "Then one day, in a marsh of the Ganges, the wise king bathed in the Ganges and headed back to the ashram. A wind then started to blow, and a great forest fire blazed up. It burned that entire forest, overwhelming it completely. The herds of wild animals that were being burnt all around, and the two-tongued snakes and the herds of boars, came to take refuge by lying in the water. When the forest was all aflame, and utter destruction was near, the king

---

[55] "Doorway to the Ganges," a town where the Ganges enters the plains.
[56] This means eating nothing but an evening meal every third day, the reckoning being that (there being two meals each day) the faster skips five meals without eating and has no meal until the evening of the third day.

had scant breath to make any exertion, because of his fasting, and so he was not able to run away, nor were your two emaciated mothers.

[22–27] "Then the king, seeing the fire coming close, said to Sanjaya the Bard, 'Go, Sanjaya, where the fire will not burn you at all. We have been caught here by the fire and will go to our ultimate destination.' Sanjaya, the best of speakers, replied to him in great distress, 'Your majesty, this will be an undesirable death for you, in a meaningless fire. But I don't see any means to escape the fire. Please tell me what is to be done about this right now.' The king replied, 'This death is not undesirable for us who have willingly gone forth from our home. Water, fire, and wind, as well as fasting, are approved for those who have engaged in *tapas*. Sanjaya, leave right away.'

[28–33] "Then the king settled his mind in meditation, and, facing east, he sat down with Gandhari and Kunti. When the wise Sanjaya saw him do this, he circled him to the right and said, 'Yoke yourself.' And the king, who was wise and the son of a sage,[57] did what Sanjaya said. Obstructing the cluster of his senses, he sat there like a piece of wood. And the once fortunate Gandhari, and your mother, Kunti, committed themselves to the forest fire, as did your father the king. But Sanjaya the Bard, the brilliant driver, escaped from that forest fire. I saw him on the banks of the Ganges, surrounded by hermits. He reported all of this to them and took leave of them, and then he went to the mountain Himalaya.

[34–38] "And that is how the high-minded Kuru King went to his death, your majesty, and Gandhari and Kunti, your two mothers. (By chance, as I was walking along, I happened to see the king's corpse and those of the two queens.) Then the hermits met in that *tapas* forest. And when they heard of the king's culmination and final destination, they did not grieve. I heard all of this there, your majesty, son of Pandu, how the king was burnt and the two queens. This is nothing to grieve about, your majesty. The king had a good

---

[57] Nilakantha says this is a reminder that he is Vyasa's son and therefore skilled in yoga.

end, achieving union with fire, and so did Gandhari and your mother."

[39–4] When the great-hearted Pandavas heard from this how Dhritarashtra had gone out, a great grief arose in them. And a great sound of suffering arose from the people in the inner quarters, and from the people of the city, when they heard of the king's final destination. King Yudhishthira, deeply miserable, cried out "Oh no! Oh no!" and raised his arms and wept as he remembered his mother. And so did Bhima and his brothers. Then a very great roar of weeping arose in the people of the inner quarters when they heard that Kunti had gone the same way. They all grieved for the old king, whose sons had been killed, and who had been burnt, and for Gandhari the woman of *tapas*.

[44] When that sound had died down, after a moment the Dharma King held back his tears with great fortitude and spoke.

Chapter 46: Yudhishthira Mourns for the Dead and Curses Kingship

[1–6] Yudhishthira said, "So that was the end of that great-hearted man, who was engaged in fierce *tapas*, as if he were someone with no protector, even though we his relatives were standing by. I find the final destinations of men hard to comprehend, since this son of Vichitravirya was burnt like that by a forest fire. This man who had a hundred illustrious sons with powerful arms, a king who had the strength of ten thousand elephants—he was burnt in a forest fire! Beautiful women used to fan him with palm leaves; now that the forest fire has dogged him to his death, vultures fan him. The king who was awakened from his lying down by hosts of bards and panegyrists now lies on the ground, because of my evil deeds. I do not mourn for the splendid Gandhari, though her sons were killed, for she has gone to the world of her husband, steadfast in her vow to her husband.

[7-12] "But it's Kunti I mourn for, who gave up her son's lordship and great shining wealth and chose to live in the forest. To hell with this kingship of ours! To hell with power, to hell with heroism! And to hell with the dharma of Kshatriyas! For we who are alive are dead men because of it. Best of Brahmins, Time's final destination is very subtle, since Kunti gave up the kingship and chose to live in the forest. The mother of Yudhishthira and Bhima, and of Arjuna (called "Victory")—how can she have been burnt as if she had no protector? When I think about this I am totally confused. I think it was meaningless that Arjuna the Ambidextrous Archer gratified Fire in the Khandava forest,[58] since Fire does not recognize a favor and is ungrateful. For even though the god had come to Arjuna the Ambidextrous Archer disguised as a Brahmin begging for alms, now he burned Arjuna's mother! To hell with Fire! And to hell with his notorious promise of alliance to Kunti's son Arjuna!

[13-18] "And this other matter seems to me even more troublesome, my lord, that the king's final connection was with a meaningless fire. How can that sort of death have come to the royal Kaurava sage who had such *tapas* and ruled this earth? While his fires consecrated by mantras were maintained there in the great forest, my father was overcome by a meaningless fire and went to his death. I think Kunti, so thin that her veins stood out, must have trembled and cried out in her terror, 'Oh! My little son, my Dharma King!' And as my mother cried, 'Bhima, come and save me from this danger!' the forest fire enveloped her on all sides. Even Sahadeva, Madri's heroic son, dearer to Kunti than her own sons,[59] did not rescue her."

---

[58] In an episode narrated at 1.214-219, Arjuna helped Fire to burn the great Khandava forest and all the living creatures in it, fighting against the god Indra. In return, Fire persuaded Varuna to give Arjuna his Gandiva bow and his two inexhaustible quivers.

[59] We have just seen that Sahadeva is the one who urges Yudhishthira to visit Kunti (15.29.9), who runs ahead to her as soon as they all see her (15.31.8), and who cannot bear to leave her (15.44.37).

[19–20] When they heard this, the five Pandavas, overwhelmed by misery, embraced one another and wept like ghosts at the end of the eon. The sound of the sobs of those weeping princes ricocheted off the walls of the palace and made heaven and earth weep in response. *Looking and looking at one another, remembering their mother's misfortune, the princes could not bear it and fell to the ground. Getting up again, embracing one another and weeping with unsteady voices, the Pandavas in their grief fell at the feet of the Dharma King.*

Chapter 47: Narada Explains the Fire and Yudhishthira Performs the Funerals

[1–9] Narada said, "Vichitravirya's son King Dhritarashtra was not burnt by a meaningless fire, according to what I heard there.[60] I will tell you about it. When that wise man, who was living on nothing but wind, entered the forest, he left behind the fires into which he had made sacrifices. This is what we heard. And then his sacrificial priests abandoned the fires in the unpeopled forest and went wherever they pleased. That fire then grew great in that forest, and that is the fire that set the forest ablaze. This is what the hermits told me. So, as I told you, the king met that very fire, his very own fire, on the marsh of the Ganges. This is how the sages whom I saw on the banks of the Ganges reported it to me, Yudhishthira. In this way, the king committed himself to his own fire, your majesty. You should not grieve for the king, who went to the supreme final destination. And your mother reached supreme perfection through

---

[60] This is the first of several rather fishy statements in this paragraph—"This is what I heard; everyone says; they all said . . ."—as Narada tries much too hard to establish a basis of truth for what is after all mere idle hearsay but the only evidence there is that Dhritarashtra did not in fact die in a meaningless, unconsecrated fire. Narada's story here directly contradicts the version that he himself has just told—Dhritarashtra was killed by a random forest fire. He may have gotten the idea of the sacrificial origin of the forest fire just now from Yudhishthira's statement (in 15.46.15) contrasting the king's "fires consecrated by mantras" with the "meaningless fire" that killed him.

her service to her elders; I have no doubt about this. Son of Pandu, Descendant of Kuru, you should do the libations for them, with all your brothers. This should be done here."

[10–13] Then the king, Bearer of the Yoke of the Pandavas, went out with his brothers and his wife. The people from the city and the countryside, honoring their devotion to the king, set out for the Ganges, each wearing a single garment. All the bulls of the Kurus plunged into the water, with Dhritarashtra's son Yuyutsu in the forefront, and made the libation for the great-hearted Dhritarashtra and for Gandhari and Kunti, reciting their names and lineages with the proper rituals. And then they settled down there outside the city to purify themselves.

[14–21] Yudhishthira summoned men who knew the ceremonial rules and were skilled in the performance of the rituals; he sent them to Gangadvara, where King Dhritarashtra, the Best of the Kurus, had been burnt. The king ordered the men to gather the bones of the dead right there in Gangadvara,[61] and he paid the men what they were owed. On the twelfth day, when he had been purified, the Pandava King performed the ritual for the dead ancestors according to the ritual rules and gave gifts to the Brahmins. In Dhritarashtra's name, the king gave gold and silver and cows and expensive beds. And the brilliant king gave gifts of matchless value to glorify the names of Gandhari and Kunti, for each individually. Each Brahmin received whatever he wished for, and in whatever quantity—beds, food, carriages, gems and jewelry, and riches. In the name of his two mothers, the king gave away carriages, coverlets, food, slave girls, and servant girls. And when the wise king had given those many funeral gifts, he went back to the city of Hastinapur.

[22–25] The men who had gone at the king's command gathered the bones of the dead[62] and then came back again. They told the

---

[61] Nilakantha says he instructed the men to throw the ashes into the Ganges.
[62] Nilakantha says, again, that they threw the ashes into the Ganges.

king that they had gathered up the bones of the dead and honored them with various garlands and perfumes, in accordance with the ritual texts. And when Narada, the supreme sage, had comforted dharmic King Yudhishthira, he went wherever he pleased.

[25–27] This is how, when the sons of the wise Dhritarashtra had been killed in the war, he lived for fifteen years in the city, always giving gifts to his relatives and close kinsmen and friends and his brothers and his own people, and then spent three years living in the forest. And when King Yudhishthira's kinsmen and close relatives had been killed, though he found scant pleasure in his heart, he maintained his kingdom.

Book Sixteen, *Mausala Parvan*, The Book of the Battle of the Clubs

Preface to Book Sixteen

Like Book Fifteen (the Book of Living in the Ashram), Book Sixteen eventually doubles back to the beginning. But where Book Fifteen does this halfway through, Book Sixteen does it after just one chapter and then again at the very end.

At the end of Book Fifteen, we left Yudhishthira and his brothers in Hastinapur, and we encounter them in Hastinapur now at the start of Book Sixteen. But many years have passed in the interval. In 16.1.7–9, Yudhishthira is told a much-condensed version of the events that have transpired during those years, culminating in the destruction of the Vrishnis, the people of the clan to which the Pandavas belong. In response, 16.2 opens with a question from the king to whom the bard is narrating the story in the outer frame: "How were the Andhakas, together with the Vrishnis, destroyed, and the Bhojas, too, great warriors, right before Krishna's eyes?"[1] To answer this question about Krishna's complicity, the theodicy question,[2] the narrator doubles back in time, at 16.2.3, to tell the story in eight long chapters, "in full detail" (vistarena, spread out), as his royal interlocutor requests.

---

[1] That the king in the frame asks about the Andhakas and Bhojas as well as the Vrishnis (16.2.1), when the bard has mentioned only the Vrishnis (in 16.1.7 and 16.1.9), may indicate that the Andhakas and Bhojas were automatically linked with the Vrishnis or that the fuller reference was taken from a different version of the story (see the Introduction).

[2] See the Introduction.

Both 16.1 and 16.2 begin with the following words: "When the thirty-sixth year had arrived." This is a reference to Gandhari's curse, which stipulated that thirty-six years after the utterance of the curse, Krishna would destroy his own people.[3] The repeated phrase, immediately followed in both chapters by a description of terrible omens, reminds us that the story that began in 16.1 is re-beginning in 16.2. The statement that the Vrishnis killed one another in the Battle of the Clubs is made again at the start of 16.6, when Daruka reports it to the Pandavas. And in the last line of the last chapter of the whole Book of the Clubs (16.9.38) we are told, yet again, that Yudhishthira, in Hastinapur, learned "what had happened to the people of the Vrishnis and Andhakas." This moment in which the disaster of the clubs is reported is where we had begun at 16.1.7 and again at 16.2.1—and where we will begin the following book, Book Seventeen, *The Book of the Great Departure*.

The actual story begins when Samba and some of the Vrishnis play a trick on a group of sages. The word used for the perpetrators, vira (cognate with the Latin vir), can mean a man or a male child. Young boys, even teenage boys, would be more likely than grown men both to think of this prank (which may have consisted in putting a club under Samba's sari to suggest the pregnant belly) and to carry it off, being more feminine in their appearance than grown men. Vira here therefore may designate teenagers. Nilakantha at 16.7.11 refers to them as boys, bala, and I have called them boys. The Jain version of the story (see the Introduction) describes the boys as "playing," another clue to their youth. Yet they are old enough to get drunk and participate in the slaughter that takes place not long after the sages predict it here. Though, earlier in the Mahabharata (15.15–16), Samba is the name of a Brahmin who makes an important speech in the assembly, I am assuming here that Samba is a teenage boy.

---

[3] 11.25.40–42; see the Introduction.

Chapter 1: Yudhishthira Sees Omens and Learns about the Battle of the Clubs

[1–6] In the thirty-sixth year, Yudhishthira, Joy of the Kauravas, saw perverse omens.[4] Harsh winds blew, bringing hurricanes and raining pebbles; vultures made circles from the right to the left.[5] The great rivers flowed backward, and fog covered the quarters of the sky. Meteors fell from the sky to the earth, raining coals. Dust covered the orb of the sun, and at sunrise the sun always appeared without any rays but clouded over with headless torsos.[6] Hideous haloes appeared around the moon and sun, tri-colored—tawny and ash-colored, with dark, rough edges. These and many other portents foretelling danger[7] were seen day after day, making hearts tremble.

[7–11] After some time, Yudhishthira, King of the Kurus, heard that the circle of the Vrishnis had been slaughtered in the Battle of the Clubs. And hearing that Vasudeva's son Krishna had been finally freed,[8] and Balarama,[9] too, Pandu's son Yudhishthira assembled his brothers and asked, "What shall we do?" When they

---

[4] Perverse (*viparitani*), literally upside-down, inverted. The word for omens, *nimittani*, also means causes, or things caused. The bad omens in this chapter recall those described at several other moments in the *Mahabharata*, particularly at the beginning of the great battle, 6.2.17 to 6.3.42.

[5] The left is the sinister or wrong direction. It is generally auspicious to circle toward the right, keeping the circled object on the right. Vultures, which prey on corpses, are birds of ill omen.

[6] The sun seems to have *kabandha*s, which can designate either headless torsos or obscuring clouds shaped like headless torsos. One might normally choose the reading of clouds for the *kabandha*s around the sun, but given the present context, replete with macabre and grisly omens, actual corpses may be at the very least a significant overtone. The verb is passive; these things "were seen." It is not clear whether they were real or merely an illusion in the minds of the beholders. These headless corpses recur at 16.3.11.

[7] The word *bhaya* can mean "danger" or "fear," again blurring the line between physical and mental signs and phenomena.

[8] To be "finally freed" (*vimukta*) here means to die; it may, in some texts, mean to find final freedom (*moksha*) from rebirth, but that does not seem to be implied in this text.

[9] Here, as often, Krishna's older brother, Balarama, is just called Rama, though he is not the Rama of the *Ramayana*, who is never mentioned in this part of the *Mahabharata*. In this translation, to avoid confusion, he will always be called Balarama.

heard that the Vrishnis, overpowered by the Brahmins' curse, had attacked one another and been destroyed, the Pandavas were shattered by distress. They did not believe that Vasudeva's son Krishna could be dead; the destruction of the Bearer of the Horn Bow was like the drying up of the ocean. When they heard about the Battle of the Clubs, the Pandavas sat down together, filled with grief and sorrow, despondent, their hopes shattered.

Chapter 2: The Sages Curse the Vrishnis and the Club Appears

[2] When the thirty-sixth year had arrived, a great disaster befell the Vrishnis. Driven by Time,[10] they killed one another with clubs.

[4–12] Sarana[11] and some other young men saw that Vishvamitra, Kanva, and Narada rich in *tapas* had come to Dvaraka.[12] In the grip of the curse of fate, they dressed Samba[13] up like a woman, put him in front of them, approached the sages and said, "This is the wife of Babhru,[14] a man of immeasurable brilliance, who wishes to have a son. You sages should certainly know this: what will she give birth to?" The sages were outraged[15] by the attempted deception. Listen to what they said in reply: "Samba here, the heir of Vasudeva's son Krishna, will give birth to a terrible iron club that will destroy the Vrishnis and Andhakas, a club with which you cruel malefactors, when you are suddenly overcome by vengeful pride, will chop

---

[10] *Kala* means "time," "death," "fate," and "doomsday." (See the Introduction.) The Vrishnis are impelled by Gandhari's curse from the past but also by the Brahmins' present curse, as well as by fate and by the fact that their time is up, all contained in the pregnant word *kala*.

[11] A son of Vasudeva, hence a brother of Krishna.

[12] The city of the Vrishnis, on the shore of the western ocean, the Arabian Sea. The name means "The Little Door," presumably between the ocean and the land of India.

[13] The son of Krishna and Jambavati (the daughter of a monkey chief).

[14] A prominent member of Krishna's family, the Yadavas.

[15] The verb, *dhrish*, here translated as "to outrage," also means "to dare to attack" but means "to rape" when applied to a woman (as "outrage" once did in English).

down the entire family, except for Balarama and Krishna the Exciter of Men. The glorious Balarama, Whose Weapon is the Plow, will abandon his body and go into the ocean;[16] and Old Age will cut down the great-hearted Krishna when he is lying on the ground."[17] This is what the sages said, looking at one another with eyes red with anger, when those miscreants had played that trick on them. And then they went to Long-haired Krishna.[18]

[13–14] When Krishna, the Subduer of Madhu, heard about all that, he knew how it would end, for he was wise, and he said to the Vrishnis, "It is to be in just that way." Then Spike-haired Krishna went back into his house. He was the ruler of the universe; he did not wish to change what already had a predetermined end.[19]

[15–20] On the next day, Samba actually gave birth to that club, a great figure of a servant[20] for the destruction of the Vrishnis and Andhakas. *It was the club by which the men in the family of the Vrishnis and Andhakas would be burnt to ashes.* They announced to King Ahuka[21] that this horrible thing had been born, as the result of a curse, and the king, looking worried, had it reduced to a fine powder. The king's men threw it into the ocean, as he commanded; *the powder they placed in the great ocean was reborn as eraka grasses.*[22] And they proclaimed in the city, in accordance with the words of King Ahuka: "From today, in all the houses of the Vrishnis and Andhakas here, all those who dwell in the city are forbidden to make wine or beer.[23] And if any man, no matter who, no matter

---

[16] 16.5.11–15.

[17] 16.5.20.

[18] Nilakantha says the sages went to him mentally, saying, "We gave the curse; forgive us."

[19] The phrase "what already had a predetermined end" can also mean "the inevitable result of past actions." Krishna said the same thing, in slightly different words, when he first heard Gandhari's curse, in book 11. (See the Introduction).

[20] Nilakantha says that "a servant" (*kimkara*) means "a messenger of Yama," the god of the dead. The word can also refer to a particular kind of an ogre (Rakshasa).

[21] Ahuka, the king of the Vrishnis and Andhakas, ruling in Dvaraka, was Krishna's great-grandfather.

[22] Nilakantha says (at 16.2.2) that atoms of the club stuck to blades of *eraka* grass.

[23] Here the text implies another point in the story that seems to have been omitted in this telling: the Brahmins' curse stated, or implied, that the vengeful pride that was to

where, should, unknown to us, make strong drink, he must impale himself alive on a stake, together with his relatives." After that all the men, knowing the great-hearted king's command, obeyed that rule, out of fear of the king.

Chapter 3: Evil Omens Appear and Krishna Proclaims a Pilgrimage

[1-7] While the Vrishnis and Andhakas were making these efforts, Time constantly prowled around all their houses. He had the form of an enormous man, deformed, bald, black and tawny.[24] He looked into the houses of the Vrishnis, but he himself was never seen.[25] *The man had black and tawny eyes and appeared in the midst of a crowd, with a great banner and with earrings made of China roses, adorned with crows' feathers, and riding on a lizard. Great archers attacked him with arrows by the hundreds of thousands, but he could not be pierced, for he was the death of all creatures.* Great winds arose day after day, terrifying, frequent, and hair-raising, for the destruction of the Vrishnis and Andhakas.[26] The highways were crawling with enormous rats, and the water jugs[27] shattered; thrushes[28] kept crying "Chichikuchi" in the houses of the Vrishnis, and the sound did not die down by day or night.[29] *Rats ate the hair and nails of*

---

overcome the Vrishnis would be excited by drunkenness. Wine plays a central role in the Jain version of the story; see the Introduction.

[24] Yama, the king of the dead, is black and tawny, and the *Mahabharata* regards bald-headed men, who might be Jain or Buddhist monks, as bad luck.
[25] Nilakantha says that Time took the form of such creatures as a dove or an owl, and that Time himself was seen in some places in an enormous form or some other form, but sometimes not seen, as he looked into houses and wandered around.
[26] These and several of the following omens are bad things in themselves but also portend other bad things.
[27] Clay jugs set by the side of the road to provide water for travelers.
[28] *Sarika*, Turdus salica, according to the dictionaries; a kind of thrush.
[29] It is not clear to me whether the birds are making an unusual, and hence inauspicious, sound, or whether their usual sound is rendered inauspicious (as well as murdering sleep) by taking place inside rather than outside the houses.

sleepers in the night. Cranes imitated the hooting of owls, and goats imitated the howling of jackals. Pale pigeons with red feet wandered through the houses of the Vrishnis and Andhakas, driven by Time. Donkeys were born in cows, and camels in female mules, cats in bitches, and mice in female mongooses.

[8–15] Then the Vrishnis committed evil acts without feeling any shame; they despised Brahmins, and the ancestors, and even the gods. They also had contempt for the elders, except for Balarama and Krishna. Wives were unfaithful to their husbands, and husbands to their wives.[30] Fires flared up and circled to the left, shooting out separate rays, some blue, some red, and some crimson as madder dye. In that city, men repeatedly saw the sun surrounded by headless corpses at rising and setting.[31] When food was completely cooked and perfectly prepared in the kitchens, worms were seen in it just as it was being served. When people were wishing one another good day and great-hearted people were chanting, the sound of people running toward them was heard, but no one was seen. *Ear-shattering howls of dogs were heard everywhere.* Everyone saw someone else's zodiac sign being struck by planets again and again, but never their own.[32] When Krishna's conch sounded in the houses of the Vrishnis and Andhakas, donkeys brayed in response, making a horrible noise all around them.

[16–20] Spike-haired Krishna, seeing that Time had now twisted in this way,[33] and realizing that the new moon day was on the inauspicious thirteenth day of the month,[34] said this to them: "The planet of eclipse has made the fifteenth lunar day the fourteenth day again; it happened then in the war of the Bharatas, and again today

---

[30] A rare moment of sexual equality in ancient India, however negative.

[31] We met these headless corpses at 16.1.4.

[32] Nilakantha says that they did not see their very own constellation, pointing to their own death.

[33] The term *kala-paryaya* means both that Time is twisting back—that a curse from the past has come forward to work its effect now—and that Time has become twisted, perverse. See the Introduction.

[34] It's a day earlier than it should be. Nilakantha says this means that it fell in the (inauspicious) dark fortnight.

for our destruction."[35] As Krishna the Exciter of Men, the Subduer of Keshin, mused and worried about Time in this way, he realized that the thirty-sixth year had arrived: "What Gandhari said out of her pain, when her relatives had been killed and she was burning with sorrow for her sons, that is what has now come about. And what is happening now is what Yudhishthira spoke of before, when the armies were marshalled and he saw terrible portents:[36] *'The best thing to do would be to give worthy gifts, offer oblations of pacification, and do good deeds.'"*

[21–22] When Vasudeva's son had said this and wished to make it come true exactly,[37] he ordered a pilgrimage. By the command of Long-haired Krishna, the king's men proclaimed there: "You must make a pilgrimage to the ocean."

Chapter 4: The Vrishnis Go on a Pilgrimage and a Fight Breaks Out

[1–5] A black woman[38] with pale teeth entered Dvaraka in the night and ran around, laughing, robbing the women in their dreams.[39]

---

[35] The meaning seems to be that since one of the bright nights suitable for ritual was a lunar eclipse (caused when the planet Rahu gobbles up the moon), they were short one ritual day at this point. Nilakantha explains the astronomical complexities: in the preceding fortnight, the waxing fortnight, there should have been an increase in the bright days of the moon, but that did not happen; on the contrary, one *tithi* (one of the fifteen lunar days of that half of the month) was lacking, for an eclipse occurred on it.

[36] In 6.19, as the battles are arrayed, evil portents appear, and Yudhishthira loses heart; this has been alluded to in verse 17 and again here. But Yudhishthira makes no prediction, there or anywhere else in the extant texts of the *Mahabharata*. Some manuscripts, however, tell us what they think he said then (the sentence included here in italics).

[37] A fine example of the double-edged, open-ended quality of fate: because Krishna knows the baneful result of the evil planetary situation *must* happen, he works to *make* it happen.

[38] Kali—the goddess of Time and Death—in the form of a woman, or just a black woman (*kali* means black).

[39] Nilakantha says that the black woman, or Kali, stole such things as the auspicious twisted thread that a woman wears from the time of her wedding. But the word for "dream" (*svapna*) can also mean "sleep," and so, in keeping with the ongoing blurring of real and imagined horrors, and the reality status of dreams in Indian thought, the verse may mean that she actually robbed the women in their sleep. The same ambiguity

Terrifying vultures devoured the Vrishnis and Andhakas in their sleep in the chambers for offerings into the fire in the middle of the sacrificial ground in their homes. Monstrous, they crouched on peoples' shoulders and uttered terrifying cries. And horrible Rakshasas and Guhyakas, two-headed and four-armed, were born in the wombs of women. People saw very frightening Rakshasas stealing jewelry, umbrellas, banners, and armor. Then the discus that Fire had given Krishna,[40] made of iron with an adamantine nave, went up to the sky, right before the Vrishnis' eyes. Four superb racehorses, swift as thought, who were yoked to Krishna's divine, sun-colored chariot, carried it away and circled above the ocean right before Daruka's eyes.[41] Apsarases carried away on high the two great banners, the palm tree[42] prized by Balarama and the Garuda bird[43] prized by Krishna, the Exciter of Men, and their voices sang out, day and night, "Go on a pilgrimage!" *They went into the sky with their chariots to enter the heaven of those who enjoy the enduring pleasures of the sight and touch and love of god.*

[6–9] Then the Vrishni and Andhaka warriors, bulls among men, together with the people from the inner quarters, were ready and eager to go on a pilgrimage.[44] The Andhakas and Vrishnis prepared cooked food and raw food, and drink, and a lot of wine of various sorts, and many kinds of meat. Then the wealthy, hot-tempered

---

hedges the "sleep" in the added verse about the vultures and in the verb "saw" in the second verse.

[40] Fire (Agni) gave Krishna the discus at 1.216.21, on the occasion of the burning of the Khandava forest (cf. 15.46.11), promising him that it would always return to his hand, like a boomerang.

[41] Daruka is Krishna's charioteer; the chariot is yoked with Krishna's famous white horses.

[42] Balarama is famous for drinking palm wine, often to excess.

[43] Krishna's vehicle, his *vahana*.

[44] A religious pilgrimage or a secular pilgrimage? The latter would have been more like a picnic, with food and drink. (See the Introduction). Where the first sort of pilgrimage was ostensibly intended to protect the people of the city, the second sort would actually render the men liable to dangerous drunken behavior. Apparently the Vrishnis and Andhakas, clearly advised to choose the former, chose the latter, the wrong kind of pilgrimage, incidentally violating the king's temperance rule, too.

men, addicted to toddy,[45] went out from the city with carts, horses, and elephants. The Yadavas settled down in Prabhasa,[46] in the appropriate places and houses for each of them, with their wives and with enormous quantities of food and drink.

[10–12] Uddhava[47] was clever at politics,[48] and he knew yoga. When he learned that the men had settled down on the shore of the sea, he went to them to bid them farewell. As the great-hearted Uddhava set out, Krishna saluted him, his hands cupped in reverence. Knowing about the destruction of the Vrishnis, Tawny Krishna did not wish to hold him back. Then the Vrishni and Andhaka warriors, twisted by Time, saw Uddhava going, filling heaven and earth with his brilliance.

[13–20] The food that those great-hearted people had prepared for the sake of Brahmins they gave, now flavored with the perfume of wine, to the monkeys.[49] Those hot-tempered men held a great drinking party in Prabhasa, crowded with hundreds of musical instruments, a melee of dancers and actors. In Krishna's presence, Balarama drank with Kritavarman, and so did Satyaki,[50] Gada,[51] and Babhru. Then, in the middle of the assembly, Satyaki, mad with drink, said to Kritavarman, laughing at him and mocking him, "What man who thinks he is a Kshatriya would kill people sleeping like the dead?[52] The Yadavas cannot brook what you did,

---

[45] *Sidhu* designates any liquor fermented from sugar or molasses. Distilling was still unknown in India at this time.

[46] A city on the west coast, near Dvaraka; the present day Somanatha in Gujarat.

[47] Krishna's cousin, the son of Devabhaga the brother of Krishna's father, Vasudeva. Uddhava plays a much more important role in later Krishna mythology.

[48] *Artha:* politics and economics, worldly matters. Nilakantha, however, says that he was learned in matters of *moksha*.

[49] Nilakantha says that the use, in other ways, of materials designated for Brahmins is a cause of the destruction of one's lifespan. In the *Bhagavata Purana*, centuries later, the young Krishna famously threw butter to the monkeys, but this was laughed away as childish mischief.

[50] A Vrishni cousin of Krishna.

[51] A younger brother of Krishna.

[52] The reference is to the night raid in the *Sauptikaparvan* (Book Ten), in which Kritavarman and others slaughtered their sleeping enemies.

Kritavarman." Pradyumna,[53] the best of the charioteers, applauded what Satyaki had said, insulting Kritavarman. This infuriated Kritavarman, who said to Satyaki, pointing at him contemptuously with his left hand, "How could you, a so-called hero, have brought down Bhurishravas[54] in a most cruel slaughter when his arm had been cut off in the battle and he had vowed to die!"

[21–26] When Long-haired Krishna, Killer of Enemies, heard what Kritavarman had said, he was filled with vengeful pride and looked at him sideways with an angry gaze. Then Satyaki reminded Krishna the Subduer of Madhu about the story of the Syamantaka jewel that had belonged to Satrajit.[55] When Satyabhama heard that, she became furious and ran weeping into the arms of Long-haired Krishna, Exciter of Men, rousing his fury. After that, Satyaki arose full of anger and said: "I swear this in all truth, fair-waisted woman: this foul-hearted man, the evil Kritavarman, shall go along the path traveled by Draupadi's five sons and Dhrishtadyumna and Shikhandin,[56] whom he killed in their sleep when he abetted Drona's son Ashvatthaman on the night raid.[57] Today both his lifespan and his fame are finished."

[27–33] As he said this, Satyaki ran at Kritavarman in fury and cut off his head with his sword, right in front of Long-haired Krishna. Then, as Satyaki kept killing others, too, in the same way, on all sides, Spike-haired Krishna ran at him in the hope of restraining him. And then the Bhojas and Andhakas, all of them, united as one, driven on by the twisting of Time, surrounded Satyaki to stop him. When Krishna the Exciter of Men, whose brilliance was great, saw

---

[53] A son of Krishna and Rukmini.

[54] An ally of Duryodhana. Arjuna had cut off Bhurishravas's right arm as he was about to kill Satyaki, and Bhurishravas had ritually prepared to die, but still Satyaki cut off his head. (7.117.62).

[55] The Sun god had given the Syamantaka jewel to king Satrajit; after many intrigues, Krishna ended up with both the jewel and Satrajit's daughter Satyabhama. (He married the girl and was falsely accused of having stolen the jewel). But when Babhru, a Vrishni, killed Satrajit and took the jewel from Satyabhama, Krishna let him keep it.

[56] Two warriors who died (as did Draupadi's sons) in the night raid.

[57] Ashvatthaman was the instigator of the night raid.

them attacking swiftly in their fury, he did not become angry, for he knew that it was the twisting of Time. But they, filled with the madness of drink and driven by their vengeful pride, beat Satyaki with the pots that still had their leftovers in them.[58] As they were killing Satyaki, Rukmini's son Pradyumna became angry and ran into the midst of them to rescue him.[59] Pradyumna was embroiled with the Bhojas, and Satyaki with the Andhakas; because they were outnumbered, the two of them were killed there, right before Krishna's eyes.

[34–41] When Long-haired Krishna, Joy of the Yadus, saw that they had killed his own son and Satyaki, in his fury he grabbed a fistful of *eraka* grass. That became a horrible iron club, diamond-hard, which Krishna used to kill anyone who stood in front of him. Then the Andhakas and Bhojas and the Vrishnis who were relatives of Satyaki, driven by Time, killed one another with clubs in an uproar. Whenever anyone among them grasped a blade of *eraka* grass in anger, that blade of grass then seemed to become diamond-hard. A blade of grass there seemed to become a club. (Recall that all of this was caused by the Brahmins' curse.[60]) Whatever grass they hurled then, wounding and wounding, seemed to become a solid club, diamond hard. Son killed father, and father son. Drunk, they ran around smashing one another. The Kukuras[61] and Andhakas rushed like moths into a fire. No one thought about running away even when he was being killed.

[42–46] Krishna the strong-armed Subduer of Madhu, seeing this and knowing that it was the twisting of Time, stood there, resting on a club. But when he saw that Samba was dead, and Charudeshna and Pradyumna and Aniruddha,[62] then Krishna

---

[58] Leftovers have strongly negative caste associations of pollution.
[59] Rukmini is a wife of Krishna.
[60] A rare direct comment from the bard, Vaisampayana, to his royal listener in the outer frame.
[61] Yet another ethnic group related to the Vrishnis.
[62] Charudeshna, Pradyumna, and Aniruddha are all, like Samba, sons of Krishna and Rukmini. Apparently Krishna's fury, first incited by the death of his son Samba and then

became angry. And when he saw Gada lying there, he was overwhelmed by anger, and, with his mace, antelope-horn bow and discus, he saw to it that no one remained alive.[63] Daruka and the brilliant Babhru, conqueror of enemy citadels, spoke to Krishna, Prince of the Dasharhas,[64] as he was slaughtering. Hear what they said: "Lord, Unfallen One, you have destroyed[65] almost everything. Find Balarama's trail, and let us go where he is."

Chapter 5: Krishna and Balarama Depart and Die

[1–3] Then Daruka and Babhru and Long-haired Krishna set out, following Balarama's trail, and they saw Balarama, of infinite heroic power, standing and thinking by a solitary tree. Krishna approached him and, showing his deep emotion, commanded Daruka: "Go quickly to the Kurus and tell Kunti's son Arjuna about this great slaughter of the Yadus. When he hears that the Yadavas have been killed by the Brahmins' curse, he must come here right away." Daruka went by chariot to the Kurus, his mind reeling.

[4–6] When Daruka had gone, Long-haired Krishna, seeing that Babhru was near him, said: "You must protect the women! Go quickly! Don't let bandits[66] harm them to get their treasures." At the command of Long-haired Krishna, Babhru set out, though he was suffering from drunkenness and grieving for the slaughter of his relatives. But as Babhru was hurrying along, alone, still

abated when he recalled his divine omniscience, was roused again by the sight of the death of his other sons.

[63] The Sanskrit phrase also suggests a sacrifice in which there was no remainder.
[64] Yet another ethnic group in this big family.
[65] The word used here for "destroyed" (*samhritam*) basically means "reabsorbed," introducing a metaphysical echo of the belief that the universe is reabsorbed into the creator at every doomsday, to remain latent until the next creation (called an emission, *srishti*).
[66] The Sanskrit word here, *dasyus*, means both people outside the Hindu caste world and robbers who attack in armed bands. Bandit seems the best approximation.

near Long-haired Krishna, suddenly a great club, hurled out of a hunter's concealed trap, killed him, cursed by the Brahmins.[67] When Krishna saw that Babhru had been killed, he said to his older brother: "Wait right here for me, Balarama, until I put the women under the protection of kinsmen."

[7–9] Then Krishna the Exciter of Men entered the city of Dvaraka and said to his father, Vasudeva: "You, sir, must protect our women all together and await the return of Wealth-winning Arjuna. Balarama sits waiting for me on the edge of the forest, and I will join him today. I have seen in the past this slaughter of the Yadus and the kings, the bulls of the Kurus. Today, here, I cannot look at this city of the Yadavas without the Yadus. I will go to the forest with Balarama and engage in *tapas*; know this from me." And Krishna touched his head to his father's feet and quickly went away.

[10] Then a great roar arose out of the city with its women and boys. And then Long-haired Krishna, turning back when he heard the sound of the crying women, said, "Arjuna the Ambidextrous Archer, first among men, will come to this city and free you from your sorrow."[68]

[11–15] When Long-haired Krishna went on from there, he saw Balarama standing alone in a lonely forest, engaged in yoga. Then he saw a great white cobra[69] come out of the man's mouth; as he watched, full of emotion, the cobra headed toward the great ocean. The cobra had a thousand heads with red mouths, and his expanded

---

[67] It is not clear, grammatically, whether Babhru or the club is cursed by the Brahmins; perhaps both. Nilakantha says that a club attached to an iron hammer in a trap flew by itself to Babhru because he was cursed by the Brahmins.

[68] The note on p. 48 of the critical edition points out that Krishna knows that Arjuna will not, in fact, save the women: "Krishna's present assurance to the women would seem to be inconsistent with his divine nature and omniscience. He must have, as such, known that Arjuna was not likely to save them." Yet Krishna does not promise that Arjuna will save the women's lives; he merely promises that Arjuna will free them (*mochayitri*) from their sorrow, and that he does—by leading them to their death, their freedom (*mukti*). See the Introduction for the problem of Krishna's role in the destruction of his family.

[69] More precisely, a Naga, either a cobra altogether or a cobra from the waist down, anthropomorphic from the waist up.

hood was as high as a mountain. As he left his own body,[70] the ocean received him back with honor, as did the divine cobras and the sacred rivers. Karkotaka, Vasuki, Takshaka,[71] Prithushravas, Varuna, Kunjara, Mishri, Shankha, Kumuda, Pundarika, and the cobra Dhritarashtra,[72] Hrada, Kratha, Shitikantha, and Ugratejas, and then the two cobras named Chakramanda and Atishanda, and the supreme cobra Durmukha, and Ambarisha, and even King Varuna[73] himself—rising up to meet him, they greeted him with welcome and honored him with the rituals of water to drink and water for his feet.[74]

[16–18] When his brother had gone, Krishna, Vasudeva's most brilliant son, who knew, with his divine gaze, all the final destinations, wandered around in the deserted forest, thinking, and then he rested on the ground. For Krishna remembered all that he had known before, what Gandhari had said in the past, and how Durvasas had told him to smear on himself the leftovers from the milk-rice.[75] His resolution was great as he thought about the destruction of the Andhakas and Vrishnis, and about the demise of the Kurus. He realized it was Time to move on to death, and so he obstructed his sensory powers. *Even though he was a god, and knew the truth of all matters, he wanted to make a sign in order to protect the stability of the worlds, to let Durvasas keep his word, and to*

---

[70] That is, the cobra left the body of Balarama. Balarama's soul returns to its true existence as Shesha, the serpent of eternity in the ocean; and so he leaves behind on the shore his body, the human body of Balarama.
[71] Several of these snakes, particularly the first three, have stories of their own, told elsewhere in the *Mahabharata*.
[72] The name of a famous serpent, as well as of the human Kaurava king.
[73] God of the waters.
[74] The cobra does not actually have feet, but water to wash the feet is part of the ritual of welcoming a guest, and a ritual is a ritual.
[75] Durvasas had asked Krishna to prepare for him some *payasa* (a kind of rice-pudding, made of milk, rice, and sugar), and then told him to smear the leftovers of the *payasa* all over his (Krishna's) body. But Krishna had not wanted to smear it over the soles of his feet and didn't. Only later did Durvasas assure him that he would be invulnerable wherever the mixture had touched his skin. And so Krishna was invulnerable everywhere but on his feet, like Achilles. The incident is told at *Mahabharata* 11.25 and 13.144.19–39.

free people from their doubts. When he had obstructed his sensory powers, speech, and mind, Krishna lay down and engaged in the ultimate yoga.

[19–21] Then Old Age[76] came to that place. He was a fierce hunter, hoping to get a wild animal.[77] As Long-haired Krishna was lying down, engaged in yoga, the hunter, Old Age, mistook him for a wild animal and hastily pierced him with an arrow in the sole of his foot. He went up to him, intending to lay hold of him. But then the hunter saw that it was a man engaged in yoga, wearing a yellow garment, and with several arms. Realizing that he had made a bad mistake, he touched the man's two feet with his head, his body revealing his distress. The great-hearted Krishna then consoled him and rose up, filling heaven and earth with his glory. *Because of Jara's remorse, his karma, and his birth, and because he had seen the god of infinite power, when he had left his body the gods brought him to heaven, where Krishna was worshipped by the hosts of sages.*

[22–25] When Krishna reached heaven, Indra, Lord of the Vasus, and the Ashvins and Rudras and Adityas and the Vasus and the All-gods came up to meet him and so did the sages and perfected beings, and the chief Gandharvas with the Apsarases. Then Krishna Narayana, the Lord of Fierce Brilliance, the beginning with no end, the great-hearted teacher of yoga, pervading heaven and earth with his glory, reached his own immeasurable place. The gods and the sages joined Krishna, and the celestial musicians and the best Gandharvas and finest Apsarases honored him, and the perfected beings and Sadhyas bowed to him. The gods welcomed him joyously, and the supreme sages praised the

---

[76] *Jara* means "old age." Nilakantha says this was someone of the Kaivarta (fisherman) caste, named Jara. But *jara* is a feminine noun, inappropriate for the name of a man. Evidently it is a metaphor, suggesting that Krishna apparently dies of old age just like the rest of us, that Time has come to claim even Krishna. This is an ignominious death for a great hero, not to mention an incarnate god. Indeed, Krishna is the only one of Vishnu's avatars who dies.

[77] The word *mriga* can mean either a deer or any wild animal (like *"Tier"* in German and "deer" in Old English).

Lord with words. The Gandharvas paid homage to him, praising him, and Indra the Much-invoked welcomed him joyously, with pleasure and affection.

[They said]: "We bow, we bow to you, Lord with the Bow of Horn. You revealed yourself on earth by establishing dharma. You killed all the enemies of the gods, the one called Kamsa and the others,[78] and when the earth was distressed by its burden you established it firmly.[79] Go, lord, to the divine place that never grows old and is immeasurable, difficult to know, supreme, but which can be reached by the sacred texts. Go, lord, and protect those who have fallen into misery, you who are born in your own form in eon after eon."

Then the assembly of the gods followed him in all his splendor and showered him with a rain of flowers. Speech, which had come there and taken on a form said, "Your majesty, come into the midst of the sun. This form of mine that has four arms is special and abides in heaven. When it goes to earth no worshipper can fathom it, for I dwell in heaven eternally." The gods failed to reach that place and turned back, remembering the god in their thought. Brahma and the others, the lords of gods, praising his virtues, reached their own auspicious worlds.

Chapter 6: Arjuna Goes to Dvaraka

[1–3] Daruka, meanwhile, had gone to the Kurus and had seen Kunti's sons, great warriors. He told them how the Vrishnis had destroyed one another in the Battle of the Clubs. When they heard that the Vrishnis had been destroyed, together with the Bhojas, Kukuras, and Andhakas, the Pandavas burned with grief, shaken in

---

[78] Kamsa, Krishna's mother's cousin, was the wicked king of Mathura, who tried many times to kill Krishna until Krishna finally killed him. This story is told in the tenth-century *Bhagavata Purana*.

[79] A reference to the episode often used to justify Krishna's failure to prevent the war. See the Introduction.

their hearts. Then Arjuna, the dear friend of Long-haired Krishna, received their permission to depart. Saying, "This no longer exists,"[80] he set out to see Vasudeva, his mother's brother.[81]

[4–7] When he had gone with Daruka to the dwelling place of the Vrishnis, he saw that Dvaraka was like a woman whose protector had died. For those women who had formerly been protected by the protector of the world[82] had lost their protector, and when they saw Kunti's son Arjuna as their protector, they cried out to him. The household of Vasudeva's son Krishna consisted of sixteen thousand women, from whom a great cry arose when they saw that Arjuna had arrived. When Arjuna the Heir of Kuru saw those women who had lost Krishna and their sons, he was blinded by tears and could not look at them.

[8–14] He saw Dvaraka as a horrible river, with its waters consisting of the Vrishnis and Andhakas, horses for fish, chariots for boats, the sound of musical instruments and chariots for the sound of its waves, and the houses' bathing ghats for crocodiles; with jewels for its clumps of aquatic moss and adamantine ramparts for its floating garlands; with the streaming traffic in its big streets for its whirlpools and courtyards for its still pools; and with Balarama and Krishna for its crocodiles. Dvaraka was like the Crossing-Over[83] river of death in the grasp of the noose of Time. The wise Arjuna saw the city bereft of the bulls of the Vrishnis, its glory gone, its happiness lost, like a lotus pond in winter.[84] Seeing Dvaraka like that, and Krishna's wives, Kunti's son Arjuna burst into tears and

---

[80] A cryptic remark, perhaps meaning that that there is no longer any reality in this world.

[81] Vasudeva, Krishna's father, was a brother of Kunti, Arjuna's mother. Unknown to Arjuna, Krishna has already informed Vasudeva about the slaughter (16.5.7–11).

[82] The women are all Krishna's wives. Krishna, the protector of the world, had been their protector (and husband), but now he had rendered them protectorless (widowed).

[83] The Vaitarani, the Indian version of the Greek river Styx, separates (or connects) earth and the regions of hell. This passage foreshadows both the forthcoming flooding of Dvaraka and Yudhishthira's encounter with the Vaitarani river of hell, in Book 18, Chapter 2.

[84] These water similes for the city prepare us for the coming image of the city actually and entirely flooded, like Atlantis.

fell to the ground sobbing. Then Rukmini and Satyabhama, the virtuous daughter of Satrajit,[85] fell upon Wealth-winning Arjuna and embraced him and burst into tears. They raised him up and sat him down on a golden seat; without speaking, they embraced the great-hearted man and stayed close to him.

[15] Pandu's son Arjuna praised Krishna the Finder of Cows, and talked about him, and consoled the women, and then he set out to see his maternal uncle Vasudeva.

Chapter 7: Arjuna Visits Vasudeva, Who Grieves and Vows to Die

[1–3] Arjuna, the Bull of the Kurus, saw the great-hearted Vasudeva, Celebrated by Drumbeats, lying down, burning up with sorrow for his sons. The strong-armed, deep-chested Arjuna, Kunti's son, his eyes brimming with tears, grasped the feet of that tormented man, though he himself was even more tormented. *Strong-armed Vasudeva, Celebrated by Drumbeats, killer of enemies, wanted to smell the head of his sister's son, but he could not.*[86] The strong-armed old man embraced Arjuna with his arms; weeping in great agitation as he remembered all his sons, he lamented his brothers and sons and sons' sons and daughters' sons, and his friends, too.

[4–8] Vasudeva said, "Arjuna, I look for those who conquered kings and demons[87] by the hundreds, but I do not see them here. I am still living, Arjuna, son of Kunti, because I am hard to kill; I do not die easily. The Vrishnis were destroyed through the bad behavior of those two pupils whom you always loved and respected, Pradyumna and Satyaki, that pair whom you regarded as the best chariot warriors of the Vrishnis, whom you always praised when

---

[85] Two of the chief wives, now widows, of Krishna.
[86] Smelling the head is an intimate gesture of affection, like a kiss, particularly from a parent to a child.
[87] Daityas, a class of demons.

you talked about them, as did my little son Krishna. Wealth-winning Arjuna, Tiger of the Kurus, those two were the immediate cause of the destruction of the Vrishnis. But, Arjuna, son of Kunti, I do not blame Satyaki or Kritavarman or Babhru, nor Rukmini's son Pradyumna. For a curse was the real cause of this.

[9–11] "The Lord of the Universe, who had attacked Keshin[88] and Kamsa and separated them from their bodies, and had killed Shishupala the Chedi king who was puffed up with pride, and Ekalavya the Nishada king, and the kings of Kalinga and Magadha, and the Gandharans, and the king of Kashi,[89] and the kings in the desert, and the kings of the east, and of the south, and of the mountains—he, Krishna the Chastiser of Madhu, looked at this disaster and overlooked it.[90] *For you and Narada and the sages should recognize that Krishna the Finder of Cows is the eternal, supreme god, the Unfallen. He, the lord, my little son, Born Under an Axle,*[91] *saw the destruction of his relatives himself, and always disregarded it. The lord of the universe certainly did not wish to make otherwise now what had been said by Gandhari and by the sages. Right before your eyes, Arjuna, Heater of Foes, he brought your grandson back to life with his brilliance when Ashvatthaman had killed him.*[92] But your friend did not wish to protect these, his own relatives.

[12–18] "And so, when he saw his sons and grandsons and brothers and his friends lying slain, he said this to me: 'Today, bull among men, this family has come to this ending. Arjuna the Disdainful will come to this city of Dvaraka. You must tell him about this great slaughter that happened to the Vrishnis, and when

---

[88] Keshin was a demon in the form of a horse that Krishna killed.
[89] For the death of Ekalavya, see 7.156.19 ff. Nilakantha identifies the king of Kashi (Varanasi) as Paundrika.
[90] The verb (*abhyupeksh*) has these two meanings. Nilakantha, commenting on a slightly different reading (*anayāt* for *anayam*), "because of the disaster," says: "The disaster consisted of the offense of the boys. Even though Krishna was capable of averting the destruction of the family, he simply witnessed it, because of the disaster."
[91] It's a long story, told in later Sanskrit texts devoted to Krishna.
[92] Vasudeva is referring here to Krishna's revival of Parikshit, the son of Arjuna's son Abhimanyu (in 10.16).

that man of great brilliance has heard of the disaster of the Yadus, he will come here very quickly. I have no doubt about this. Know that I am who Arjuna is, and Arjuna is who I am.[93] Do exactly what he says. Understand this, Vasudeva, Descendant of Madhu. When your Time has come, Arjuna the Disdainful, Pandu's son, will perform your funeral ceremony among the women and children. And when Wealth-winning Arjuna has gone back, the ocean will immediately flood this city, ramparts and watchtowers and all. For, in some sacred place, together with the wise Balarama, I will restrain my life forces and immediately end my own Time.'

[19–22] "When Spike-haired Krishna, the lord of unimaginable heroism, had said this and then left me with the little boys, he went off in some direction or other. And I, here, thinking about those two great-hearted brothers and about the horrible slaughter of our relatives—I do not eat anything and am emaciated with sorrow. And I will not eat, and I will not live. It is fortunate that you have come, Arjuna, son of Pandu, son of Kunti. Do everything that Krishna said, all of it. This kingdom is yours, Arjuna son of Kunti, and these women and treasures, Subduer of Enemies. For I will give up these my dearest life's breaths."

Chapter 8: Arjuna Leads the Vrishni Women out of Dvaraka and Bandits Attack

[1–8] Out of his own melancholy heart, Arjuna the Disdainful answered his uncle Vasudeva, whose heart was suffering: "I can't bear to look at the earth here for long, uncle, now that the Madhus and the Vrishni hero, Krishna, have left it, my lord. The six of us—King Yudhishthira, Bhima, Sahadeva, Nakula, and I, Arjuna the son of Pandu, and Draupadi—are of one mind: surely the Time

---

[93] The argument is that since Arjuna is identical with Krishna, Arjuna can perform the death rituals that Krishna would normally do.

has now come for the king to move on to another world. You, who understand Time better than anyone, must know that this Time has come. But I will somehow collect all the Vrishni women and children and old people and have them led to Indraprastha." Then Wealth-winning Arjuna said to Daruka: "I wish to see the counselors of the Vrishnis, without delay." And then, mourning for the warriors, the hero Arjuna entered the Yadavas' assembly, called "Good Dharma."[94] When he had taken his seat there, all the ministers, Brahmins, and Vedic scholars surrounded him and stood near him.

[9–14] They were all silent, their hearts wretched and their minds reeling. Though Kunti's son Arjuna himself was even more wretched, he said to them: "I myself will lead the people of the Vrishnis and Andhakas to Indraprastha. But the ocean will flood this entire city. Make ready your vehicles and various precious possessions. Vajra[95] here will be your king in Indraprastha. On the seventh day, when the sun rises clear at daybreak, we will all be staying outside the city. Make ready without delay!" When Kunti's son, tirelessly working, had addressed the people of the city in this way, they made ready quickly, anxious for their own survival. Kunti's son Arjuna spent that night in the home of Long-haired Krishna, suddenly overwhelmed by the great delusion of sorrow.

[15–18] The next morning, Vasudeva, Heir of Shuri, blazing with inner heat and great brilliance, yoked himself with yoga and went to his ultimate destination. Then Vasudeva's house rang with the great and terrible sound of women lamenting and weeping. All the women let their hair down loose, threw off their jewelry and garlands, beat their breasts with their hands, and lamented piteously. Devaki and Bhadra and Rohini and Madira, the best of wives, decided to climb on the pyre after their husband.

---

[94] The epithet (Sudharma) is also a name of the assembly hall of the gods.
[95] Krishna's great grandson, son of Aniruddha son of Pradyumna son of Krishna.

[19–27] Then Kunti's son Arjuna had Shura's son Vasudeva carried out on a great carriage harnessed with men and profusely garlanded. All the people who lived in the city of Dvaraka, assailed by grief and sorrow, followed him wherever he went. The umbrella from his horse sacrifice and his blazing sacrificial fires and sacrificial priests went in front of that carriage, and his queens followed him, well adorned, surrounded by thousands of wives and thousands of daughters-in-law. In a spot that the great-hearted man had been fond of when he was alive, they settled him and performed the sacrifice for the ancestors. When Shura's son Vasudeva was on the funeral pyre, those four of his wives, fine women, climbed up after him, going to the world of their husband. Pandu's son Arjuna had Vasudeva with his four wives burned with sandalwood and fragrances arranged above and below. Then the sound of the ignited fire arose, and the singing of the Vedic chants and the men weeping. And then all the young Vrishni men, led by Vajra, together with the wives of great-hearted Vasudeva, performed the libation rites.

[28–31] When the Ruddy Arjuna, who never lapsed in his fulfillment of dharma, had had them perform that dharmic act, he went where the Vrishnis had been destroyed. When Arjuna the Heir of Kuru saw them there, fallen in the slaughter, he became even more deeply unhappy, and he did what was appropriate to the Time. According to their eminence, he performed all the rituals for those who had been slain by the clubs that had grown out of *eraka* grass because of the Brahmins' curse. Then he searched for the bodies of Balarama and Vasudeva's son Krishna and had them burnt by men properly trained for that task.

[32–39] When Pandu's son Arjuna had performed their death rituals according to the rules, on the seventh day he mounted his chariot and quickly set out. And, on carriages yoked with horses or with bullocks, donkeys, or camels, the wives of the Vrishnis, weeping, emaciated with grief, followed the great-hearted, Wealth-winning Arjuna, Pandu's son. The servants of the Andhakas and Vrishnis, riding astride or in wagons, and the people from the city and the country, they went too, as Kunti's son Arjuna had commanded, encircling the group of women who had lost their protectors and had only old men and children with them. Those mounted on elephants like mountains were flanked by reserve troops and by armed men who protected the elephants' feet. All the sons of the Andhakas and Vrishnis followed Kunti's son Arjuna devotedly—Brahmins, Kshatriyas, Vaishyas, and wealthy Shudras. The sixteen thousand women in the harem of Vasudeva's son Krishna went behind Vajra, wise Krishna's great-grandson. And many thousands and millions and billions of the women of the Bhojas and Vrishnis and Andhakas went out, women whose protectors had been killed. Kunti's son Arjuna, the best of charioteers, conqueror of enemy citadels, guided that circle of the Vrishnis, a veritable ocean of people with great wealth.

[40–41] When the people had gone out, the waters of the ocean that is the home of sea monsters flooded Dvaraka, which was still full of precious things. *The ocean flooded with its water whatever piece of land Arjuna, the tiger among men, left. And the ocean told all the living creatures there: "Leave the piles of gold and the golden bowls and the various jewels and various golden things. Leave your most valuable material goods here all together, undivided. I will now protect this city of Vishnu, with all its houses, where, in the Golden Age, there will again be an avatar.*[96] *I will oversee the treasure of this man and that, and all the things that are our wealth."* Watching that marvel, the people who had lived in Dvaraka went faster and faster, saying, "Alas! It is fate."

[42–48] Wealth-winning Arjuna led the Vrishni women, camping in pleasant groves and on mountains and beside rivers.

---

[96] This rather cryptic prophecy seems to refer to a moment in the future when the world will be recreated after the apocalyptic flood and begin again with another Golden Age or Winning Age or First Age, the Krita Yuga; at that time Vishnu will assume several aquatic avatars: as a fish, a tortoise, and an aquatic boar. Perhaps one of these will visit the submerged Dvaraka. For further versions of the myth of the flooding of Dvaraka, see Doniger, *The Hindus*, 54–60.

When the wise lord reached the prosperous Land of Five Rivers,[97] he settled down in a spot rich in oxen, cattle, and grain. But when bandits saw that Kunti's son Arjuna, all alone, was leading the women whose husbands had been killed, their greed was aroused. And those unsavory-looking, evil-doing Abhiras,[98] their minds undone by greed, got together and plotted: "This warrior Arjuna, all alone except for these fighters whose fighting days are over, is leading old men and children whose protectors have been killed, and they're trespassing on our territory. *His pride swells because he killed Bhishma and Karna and Jayadratha, and now, scorning us who have cudgels in our hands, the fool underestimates us. He killed people led by Bhishma and Drona even though they had taken off their armor, and he defeated Indra and Rudra, and today he insults us.*" Then those bandits, by the thousands, with cudgels for their weapons, ran against the people of the Vrishnis to steal the plunder. Routing the common people with a great lion's roar, they fell upon them for their wealth, driven by the twisting of Time.

[49–54] Arjuna, Kunti's strong-armed son, turned back suddenly with his foot-followers and said to the bandits, smiling, "Turn back, unless you want to die, you who do not know what dharma is. Don't suffer and die now, broken by my arrows." The fools ignored his speech and attacked the people, even though he tried again and again to stop them. Then Arjuna tried to stretch his great divine bow named Gandiva, which never wore out, but he could barely do it, and only with effort. *With all his strength, Arjuna the Victorious was not able to bend it.* He managed to string it with difficulty in the midst of all the confusion and tumult, and he thought of his mantric weapons, but he could not even remember them.[99] *The Gandhiva*

---

[97] The Punjab, watered by five rivers, the present Sutlej, Beas, Ravi, Chenab, and Jhelum.

[98] A tribal people who lived in the Punjab area.

[99] Arjuna had obtained from the gods several mantric weapons, magic words that, in the past, he had had merely to think of in order to destroy many enemies. Now he can no longer recall them.

bow became loose again, and the arrows shot from it were not able to pierce the skin. Seeing such great deterioration in the manly power of his two arms in the fight, and the loss of his great divine weapons, he became ashamed.

[55–61] All the Vrishni warriors, on their elephants and horses and chariots, were not able to stop the people as they were being stolen away, because there were so many women running this way and that. Kunti's son Arjuna made an effort to rescue the people, but the most attractive women were abducted on all sides, right before the warriors' eyes, and others went away willingly. Then Wealth-winning Arjuna, Kunti's son, the lord, together with his Vrishni followers, killed the bandits in a great fury, with arrows shot from his Gandiva bow. But in a moment, his arrows that always flew straight were exhausted. The arrows that were never exhausted before, drinking the blood of wounds, were exhausted now. When he had used up all his arrows, Arjuna, the son of Indra the Chastiser of Paka, was overwhelmed by grief and sorrow; then he killed the bandits with the tip of his bow. But the barbarians took the women of the Vrishnis and Andhakas and went away in all directions, right before the eyes of Kunti's son Arjuna.

[62–69] Wealth-winning Arjuna thought in his mind and heart that it was fate. Filled with grief and sorrow, the lord did nothing but sigh. The loss of his magical weapons and the waning of the manly power of his arms and the uselessness of his bow and the exhaustion of his arrows broke the heart of Kunti's son Arjuna. Thinking, "It's fate," he turned away and said, "This no longer exists."[100] Then that high-minded man took down into the Field of the Kurus the remainder of the women, who had lost most of their jewels. That is how Wealth-winning Arjuna, the Heir of Kuru, led the women of the Vrishnis, those who were left after the others had been abducted, and had them settle down here and there. Kunti's son Arjuna, the best of men, settled Kritavarman's son there in the

---

[100] He had made the same cryptic remark at 16.6.3.

city of Martikavat with the wives of the king of the Bhojas, those who were left after the others had been abducted. And then, taking the old people and children and the women, all of whom who had lost their men, Pandu's son Arjuna settled them in Indraprastha. The dharmic Arjuna settled Satyaki's beloved son on the Sarasvati River, with the old people and the children.

[70–74] Arjuna, the killer of enemy heroes, gave the kingship in Indraprastha to Vajra. But Babhru's wives went away,[101] though Vajra tried to hold them back. Then the Gandharan princess Rukmini, Shibi's daughter Haimavati, and Queen Jambavati entered the fire. And Satyabhama and Krishna's other honored queens agreed together in the decision to engage in *tapas* and entered the forest. *Eating fruits and roots and so forth, intent only upon meditating upon Tawny Vishnu, they crossed beyond the Himalayas and entered the village of Kalapa.* As for the men who had lived in Dvaraka and had followed Kunti's son Arjuna, called Victory, he handed them over to Vajra, dividing them up according to their worth. And when Arjuna had done what was proper for that Time, through eyes obscured with tears he saw Vyasa of the Island seated in his ashram.

Chapter 9: Arjuna Visits Vyasa and Yudhishthira

[1–6] Arjuna entered the ashram of Vyasa, Satyavati's son, and saw the sage seated in a lonely spot. He went up to this man who spoke truth and knew dharma and had taken a great vow, stood beside him, and addressed him, announcing his name: "I am Arjuna." "Welcome to you," and, "Sit down," said Satyavati's son, the great sage. When Vyasa, whose soul was at peace, saw that the mind of

---

[101] The verb is the same used earlier to describe the women who went away with the Abhiras of their own desire, while other women were being forcibly abducted. But it may simply mean that they went into the forest.

Kunti's son Arjuna was unsatisfied and discouraged, and that he was sighing again and again, he said: *"Have you been sprinkled by water from nails, hair, the end of a garment, or a pot?*[102] Have you attacked someone whose father was unmanly?[103] Have you killed a Brahmin? Or have you been conquered in battle? Because you seem to have lost your luster. I can hardly recognize you. What is this? If it is something I should hear, son of Kunti, you should tell me right away." *Then Kunti's son, sighing, said, "Listen, my lord," and told Vyasa accurately all about his own defeat.*

[7–14] Arjuna said: "The glorious Krishna, whose body was dark as a cloud, with eyes like giant lotuses, has left his body and gone to heaven with Balarama. *When I remember that, I become constantly confused and grieved, and a desire to die constantly arises in me. Remembering the ambrosial happiness of looking at, touching, and talking intimately with that great-hearted god of gods, I grow faint.* The hair-raising massacre of the Vrishnis in the Battle of the Clubs at Prabhasa, caused by the Brahmins' curse, brought about the end of the heroes. Those great-hearted heroes with their great strength, proud as lions, the Bhojas and Vrishnis and Andhakas—they killed one another in a fight, good Brahmin. They who had arms like iron bars, and could endure maces, iron bars, and spears, were slain by blades of *eraka* grass. See the twisting of Time! Five hundred thousand of those men famous for their strong arms were slaughtered when they attacked one another. As I keep thinking about the destruction of those Yadus of immeasurable vigor, and of the glorious

---

[102] Nilakantha glosses the last term as "a mouth." All of these questions imply that Arjuna has somehow been polluted, which would explain his wretched condition.

[103] This question is right on target: Arjuna had fought with lowly bandits, as well as being conquered in a shameful battle (as Vyasa goes on to guess). The critical edition lists several widely differing manuscript readings here, including, "Have you been injured by Abhiras?" Nilakantha offers a very different reading here and glosses his text as, "Have you had sex with a menstruating woman?" He reminds us that one shouldn't have intercourse with a woman for three days after the time of the flow of her blood, and he goes on to say that this is one of seven reasons for a man to have lost his luster (*shri*). The critical edition notes (on p. 49 of the *Mausala Parvan*) that this reading "(of which the commentator gives a word for word explanation not at all appropriate to the context) has therefore to be rejected."

Krishna, I cannot bear it. Like the ocean drying up,[104] a mountain moving, the sky falling, or fire chilling, I think the destruction of Krishna with his bow made of horn is impossible to believe. And without Krishna, I do not wish to remain here in the world.

[15–18] "And listen, you who are a Brahmin so rich in *tapas*, to something else even worse than this, something that shatters my heart as I think of it again and again. Right before my eyes, the Abhiras who live in the Land of Five Rivers pursued the wives of the Vrishnis in battle and abducted them by the thousands. When I took up my bow there, I was not able to stretch it fully, and the manly power of my two arms was not what it had been before. My various weapons were lost, great sage, and my arrows were exhausted in a single moment, all around me. *That bow, and those weapons, and the chariot, and the prize-winning horses, all of it was shattered in a single stroke, like a gift given to someone other than a Brahmin versed in the Veda.*

[19–24] "And the four-armed[105] man with eyes wide as lotuses, whose soul cannot be measured, who carries the conch and discus and mace, the dark one who wears a golden garment, who goes with great splendor in front on my chariot, burning the armies of the enemies—I do not see him today. The one who burnt the enemy armies with his blazing brilliance as he went in front, while behind him I would destroy them with arrows released from my Gandiva bow—when I do not see him, my spirits sink, and I seem to whirl around; my wits become faint, best of men, and I find no peace. I cannot bear to live without the heroic Krishna, Exciter of Men; for as soon as I heard that Vishnu was gone, I was so bewildered I couldn't tell east from west, north from south. Please, best of men,

---

[104] This same metaphor was used at the beginning of this same story, at 16.2.10, in the same way. Book 16 is beginning to curl back up toward its beginning.

[105] Nilakantha says that this very form of Krishna, four-armed, is always within Arjuna's view, and that it is because of this that, right after his vision of Vishvarupa (in the *Bhagavad Gita*, 11.46), Arjuna says, "Be four-armed, you who can be thousand-armed as you have all forms."

teach me what is best for me to do, for I have lost my relatives and my heroic power, and I am running about, empty."

[25–29] Vyasa said: "The great warriors of the Vrishnis and Andhakas were destroyed because they were burnt by the Brahmins' curse. You should not grieve for them, Tiger of the Kurus. *Portions of gods, they were born with the god of gods and went away with him. The god disregarded them in order to protect the stability of dharma.* For that had to happen in that way. It was the fate assigned to those great-hearted men, and Krishna overlooked it even though he was capable of averting it. For Krishna would even be able to change everything moving and still in the triple world, let alone the curse of wise men. *And in the past, those women were cursed by the sage Ashtavakra, who lost his temper because of their joke, and that is the reason why your strength ran out.*[106] Out of love for you, Vasudeva's four-armed, wide-eyed son, the ancient sage, went in front on your chariot, wielding the discus and mace. When he had removed the burden of the earth and set free this whole universe, he went back to his own supreme place.

[30–36] "But you, strong-armed bull among men, have done a great deed here for the gods, with the help of Bhima and the Twins.[107] Bull of the Kurus, I regard you as people who have succeeded in doing what was to be done. And this is the appropriate Time for you to go; I think that is the best thing for you to do. Strength, intelligence, brilliance, and foresight arise at Times of prosperity and disintegrate when Time becomes twisted. All of this has Time as its root, Wealth-winner. Time is the seed of the

---

[106] The critical edition notes that the *Brahmapurana*, 212.83–85, tells the story of Ashtavakra, whose name means "Crooked in Eight Places" and who said: "Since you women thought I had a deformed form and dishonored me with a joke, therefore I will give you this curse: By my favor you will obtain Krishna as your husband, but then, struck by my curse, all of you will fall into the hands of bandits." And so, because of the curse of that man of *tapas*, Ashtavakra, they got Krishna as their husband but then fell into the hands of bandits.

[107] Why does Vyasa omit Yudhishthira from his list of the Pandavas who have done the work of the gods? Perhaps he is anticipating Yudhishthira's protests against the gods, in passages yet to come.

universe. And it is Time that once again draws things together into annihilation, spontaneously.[108] Someone who becomes powerful once again becomes powerless; someone who becomes a ruler here once again is commanded by others. Your weapons did what was to be done, and today they have gone back to the place from which they had come. And they will come into your hand once again, when it will be the Time for that. It is Time for all of you, too, to go to the highest final destination; for I think this is the very best thing for you."[109]

[37–38] Kunti's son Arjuna understood the words of Vyasa, whose brilliance is immeasurable. He received permission to depart and went to the city of Hastinapur. He entered the city and found Yudhishthira and told him what had happened to the people of the Vrishnis and Andhakas.[110]

---

[108] Nilakantha says that the point is that this is no occasion for sorrow.
[109] Nilakantha says Vyasa is saying, "You too, just like the weapons, have done what had to be done."
[110] And here we join the narrative that was begun at the start of this Book of The Battle of the Clubs: Yudhishthira's reaction to the news of the slaughter of the Vrishnis and Andhakas.

Book Seventeen, *Mahaprasthanika Parvan*, The Book of the Great Departure

Preface to Book Seventeen

The title of this penultimate book uses a Sanskrit term (mahaprasthana, literally "the Great Departure") that comes to signify "departing in order to die." Nilakantha (on 17.1.2) says that the term means "to go to heaven." It is an approved method of suicide, of which several instances are attested in these final books of the Mahabharata—such as the death of a royal queen on her husband's pyre (though not his on hers) and death by starvation or meditation. King Dhritarashtra, facing his own death by fire, states clearly: "Water, fire, and wind, as well as fasting, are approved for those who have engaged in tapas." (15.45.27) Nilakantha (on 17.1.2) says that Vyasa undertook the Mahabharata *to demonstrate that* "For those who have done what was to be done, but have been swallowed up by unbearable unhappiness, giving up the body by means of the Great Departure is an acceptable thing to do."

Yudhishthira walks right up to heaven, but he is the only one who does this; his brothers and Draupadi fall along the wayside, each brought down by a different trivial character flaw: partiality, intellectual arrogance, vanity, empty boasting, or gluttony. And even Yudhishthira must pass a test before he can enter heaven, a test that involves his loyalty and devotion to a loyal and devoted dog.

Chapter 1: The Pandavas Install the Kings, Depart, and Encounter Fire

[1–5] And so the Pandavas heard about the Battle of the Clubs in the family of the Vrishnis and Andhakas and heard that Krishna had gone to heaven. When Yudhishthira the Kaurava King heard about the massive slaughter of the Vrishnis, he resolved upon the Departure and said to Arjuna: "Time ripens all beings, Arjuna. I am thinking about renouncing action;[1] you too, a very wise man, should consider this." "Time, Time,"[2] said Arjuna, Kunti's heroic son, agreeing with what his eldest brother had said. And when Bhima and the Twins learned of the idea that Arjuna the Ambidextrous Archer had expressed, they assented to it.

[6–9] Then, as Yudhishthira prepared to set out to engage in *tapas* through his desire for dharma,[3] he had Yuyutsu brought forth and entrusted the entire kingdom to him, the son of a Vaishya woman.[4] But when King Yudhishthira, Pandu's oldest son, had anointed[5] Parikshit as king in his own kingdom,[6] he was tormented by grief, and he said to Subhadra, "This son of your son[7] will be the king of the Kurus, and Vajra, the remainder[8] of the Yadus, has been

---

[1] *Karmanyasa*, "renouncing action/ritual/karma," has multiple meanings, but here primarily indicates discontinuing all rituals as well as all duties in dharma. Cf. 12.231.25: "Time ripens all beings by itself, in itself. But no one here on earth knows anyone whom Time has fully ripened."

[2] This also might be translated as, "Time is Death." Nilakantha glosses it by saying, "The repetition signifies 'constancy.' Time, that is, Death, cannot be avoided, so let it take place on this very day; why delay?"

[3] Nilakantha says he Departed because of his desire for dharma, not because he was carried away by emotion.

[4] He gave the kingdom to Yuyutsu (born to Dhritarashtra and a Vaishya wife) as regent, since the true king, Parikshit, was still a child.

[5] More precisely, he sprinkled him, a royal ceremony that is the equivalent of anointing with oil but baptizes with water.

[6] Nilakantha identifies this as the country whose capital is Hastinapur, formerly Yudhishthira's "own" kingdom and now Parikshit's.

[7] Parikshit is the son of Abhimanyu, who is the son of Arjuna and Subhadra.

[8] Parikshit's name means "leftover," as he is the only one left alive after the great destruction of his family. The parallel king, Vajra, is now also called a "remainder" in the same sense.

made their king. Parikshit in Hastinapur, and Vajra, the Yadava, in Indraprastha. You should protect King Vajra; do not set your mind on the violation of dharma."[9]

[10–13] Then Yudhishthira the Dharma King made the funeral libations for wise Krishna, Vasudeva's son, and for his old maternal uncle, Vasudeva, and for Balarama and all the others. And, ever dharmic, with his brothers he then tirelessly performed the funeral sacrifices for their ancestors, designating them according to the rules. *With care he fed sweet food to Vyasa of the Island, and to Narada, Bharadvaja, Yajnavalkya, and Markandeya rich in tapas, speaking of Tawny Vishnu and praising Krishna the Bearer of the Horn Bow.* To the chief Brahmins he gave jewels and garments and villages and horses and chariots and women[10] and cows by the hundreds of thousands. Yudhishthira, the Best of the Bharatas, revered Kripa as the guru, honored him with wealth and respect, and handed Parikshit over to him as a pupil.

[14–17] Then Yudhishthira, the royal sage, had his subjects assembled and told them everything that he himself wanted to do then. As soon as the people of the city and the country heard his speech, their minds were greatly distressed; they did not welcome that speech. They said to King Yudhishthira, "It should not be done like that." But the king did not do what they asked, for he knew the dharma of the twisting of Time. The dharmic king asked the people of the town and country for permission to leave, for he had set his mind on going, and then so had his brothers. *All at once, in an argument about the selling price of a valuable object, the desire for wealth took hold of all the ruling landowners. And, knowing that the Kali Age had arrived, Sahadeva smiled and reported to the king, "Dharma*

---

[9] After winning the kingdom back, now Yudhishthira is reconciled with his cousins and gives half of it back to them. One might think that the violation of dharma against which Yudhishthira is cautioning Subhadra would be to seize the other half of the kingdom for her own grandson, Parikshit. But Nilakantha is surely right in suggesting that Yudhishthira means that she should not engage in the Great Departure herself, which would violate dharma in failing to protect the two young boys, Parikshit and Vajra.

[10] Nilakantha says these were enslaved women.

has been destroyed." And the king, in low spirits, replied, "My life has ended."

[18–20] Then Yudhishthira, the Kauravya King, son of Dharma, took the ornaments off his body and put on garments made of bark. Bhima and Arjuna, and the Twins and glorious Draupadi, all put on garments of bark in the very same way. When they had had the ultimate sacrifice[11] performed according to the rules and all of them had thrown their fires away into the water, the bulls among men Departed.

[21–26] The women wept when they saw that those bulls among men had Departed, with Draupadi as the sixth, just as when they had been lost in the dice game in the past.[12] But the brothers were thrilled to be going, since they knew Yudhishthira's mind and were keenly aware that the Vrishnis had been destroyed. There were the five brothers, and Draupadi the Dark Lady as the sixth, and a dog as the seventh (all by himself, as the seventh). The king went out from Hastinapur. The city dwellers and the people of the inner quarters followed him for a long way. No one was able to say to him, "Turn back." But all the men who lived in the city turned back from there. Kripa and the others rallied round Yuyutsu. Then Ulupi, the daughter of the cobra king Kauravya,[13] entered the Ganges. And Citrangada,[14] too, went away, to the city of Manipura, and the other mothers who were left rallied round Parikshit.[15]

---

[11] Their own symbolic funerals. Nilakantha says this is the sacrifice for the final freedom (*moksha*). He adds that they placed their sacrificial fires within themselves and then they threw the fires into the waters. That is, they internalized the power of the fires with which they had performed their daily rituals and threw the mere physical element, the fire, into the water, quenching the flames.

[12] Their departure from the city after Yudhishthira lost them in a dice game (2.71.1 ff) is a close parallel, even to the people's reactions.

[13] Ulupi, daughter of a great Naga king named, confusingly, Kauravya ("descendant of Kuru," which is also the name of the Pandavas and their cousins), was a wife of Arjuna and mother of his son Iravan. As she is a water creature, she enters the river to leave earthly life.

[14] Another wife of Arjuna, daughter of Chitravahana and mother of Babhruvahana.

[15] Nilakantha says that the others were the wives of Yudhishthira, etc., and the mothers of Shrutasoma, etc.

[27–31] The great-hearted Pandavas and glorious Draupadi went forth toward the east, fasting. Engaged in yoga and committed to the dharma of renunciation, they passed through many countries and rivers and oceans. Yudhishthira went in front, and then right after him came Bhima. Arjuna followed right after him, and then the Twins, in the proper order.[16] In the rear came Draupadi the Dark Lady, the best of women, with fine hips and eyes like lotus petals. And one single dog followed the great-hearted Pandavas as they Departed in the forest. Eventually they came to the surging Blood-red Sea.[17]

[32–40] But Wealth-winning Arjuna did not let go of the celestial Gandiva bow, nor the two inexhaustible quivers,[18] because he still coveted precious things. Then they saw Fire in the form of a man standing there right before their eyes and filling the road, as if a mountain had been set down there in front of them. Fire, the God of Seven Rays, said to the Pandavas: "Hello, hello, heroic sons of Pandu! Know that I am Fire. Strong-armed Yudhishthira, and Bhima, destroyer of foes, and Arjuna, and you two sons of the Ashvins, mark my words. Best of the Kurus, I am Fire, who burnt up the Khandava forest with the power of Arjuna and Krishna Narayana.[19] This brother of yours, Ruddy Arjuna here, should give up the Gandiva bow, the supreme weapon, before he goes to the forest, where there is no use whatever for it. But the jewel of discuses that great-hearted Krishna used to have, and that has gone, will, in Time, come back into his hand again.[20] This best of bows,

---

[16] The proper order is the order of age, the eldest first.
[17] Nilakantha says that this is the ocean at the edge of the Mountain of Sunrise, the place where the sun rises. Blood-red (Lauhitya) is also the name of the Brahmaputra River.
[18] Apparently the bow and arrows, which had failed Arjuna so dramatically when he was unable to defend the women from the greedy bandits (16. 8.52–59), have magically regained their powers.
[19] On that occasion (1.214–216), Fire gave Arjuna the two inexhaustible quivers that he is now going to claim back, as well as his magic discus. The event was cited to Fire's discredit in Book Fifteen (15.46.11–12).
[20] The discus went up to heaven at 16.4.3, and at 16.9.35 Vyasa promised that it would return. Nilakantha says it will return in another avatar. "His hand" seems to refer to Krishna's hand, on the analogy of the bow and arrows going back to Varuna, as we learn in the next verse, and because it is always Krishna who has the discus.

the Gandiva, which I took from Varuna for Kunti's son Arjuna in the past, should be given back to Varuna." Then his brothers urged Wealth-winning Arjuna, and he threw that bow and the two inexhaustible quivers into the water. *A sound came from the Gandiva as it was thrown into the water, like the sound that comes out of a cloud in the sky.*

[41–44] Then Fire vanished from that spot, and the Pandavas went toward the south. They went southwest along the northern shore of the salt ocean. Then they turned again, to the west, and they saw Dvaraka, even though it had been flooded by the ocean. Then, turning again, to the north, the Best of the Bharatas went on, following the dharma of yoga, wishing to circumambulate the Earth.[21]

Chapter 2: Draupadi, Sahadeva, Nakula, Arjuna, and Bhima Fall

[1–2] Gathering in their selves, yoking themselves with yoga, they set out for the north and saw the great mountain Himalaya. *They bathed in the Brahmani River and saw the god who remains in the water, and they went to the centermost portion and saw Shiva, the mighty Rudra. They bathed at Prayaga where the five streams come together and went toward the auspicious mountain Himalaya. They bowed to Ishana and bathed in the holy Swan Water. They saw and carefully touched Kedara, the God of Gods. They offered the funeral ball of rice* (pinda), *with the proper rituals, and satisfied their ancestors and the gods. They went to the Nanda River and drank the*

---

[21] They are circumambulating the earth in the auspicious direction, always to the right, to say goodbye to it, just as they walked around their parents before saying farewell. Their voyage roughly (very roughly) follows the map of India: they start out near Hastinapur and Indraprastha (Delhi), and as they go south and southwest, they eventually go along the northern shore of the Indian Ocean. They then go west to Dvaraka (on the Arabian Sea near the present-day Mumbai) and head north toward Himalaya, passing by the desert of Rajasthan as they look toward Mount Meru, on a more mythical map.

water in the ritual manner. And so they circled on the great path and came to Himalaya. They went even beyond until they saw the ocean of sand,[22] and they gazed down upon the great Mount Meru,[23] the best of mountains.

[3-7] But as they were all moving quickly, following the dharma of yoga, Draupadi lost her yogic concentration[24] and fell to the ground. When the powerful Bhima saw that she had fallen, he looked down[25] at Draupadi with concern and spoke to Yudhishthira the Dharma King about her: "The Dark Lady never did anything against dharma, your majesty. So what has caused her to fall to the earth?"[26] Yudhishthira said: "She was very partial, especially toward Wealth-winning Arjuna. What she is experiencing today is the fruit of that." And King Yudhishthira, the son of Dharma, the wise and dharmic bull among men, went on without regarding her,[27] collecting his mind in meditation.

[8-11] Then the wise Sahadeva fell to the ground, and when Bhima saw that he too had fallen he said to the king, "This man, Madri's son, was always eager to serve us all, with no thought for himself. Why has he fallen on the earth?" Yudhishthira said, "He did not think that anyone was as intelligent as he was. This flaw in his character therefore brought about the prince's fall.[28] *[He would think], 'The secret that I have knowledge of the three Times (past, present, and future) is not publicly known. I have achieved consummate knowledge, but I will not hurt people.'"* And then Kunti's son

---

[22] That is, the desert.
[23] Meru is the mountain at the center of the earth. Apparently they are now about to start climbing up this mountain to reach heaven.
[24] Nilakantha says that her mind stumbled from her meditation.
[25] There is a triple meaning here: the verb (*aveksh*) can mean to look down at someone, to have concern for them, or just to make reference to them.
[26] There is a double meaning here, too: those who fall, fall to the ground (*mahitale*), but Draupadi is here also said to fall to the earth (*bhuvi*) instead of going on to heaven.
[27] The verb (*anavekshya*), like the negative form of our "regard" or "look/overlook," means both that he did not think about her and that he did not look at her. Nilakantha says that he disregarded her by thinking, "Let there be no affection, which would be an obstacle to entering heaven."
[28] Nilakantha remarks that even pride in one's wisdom is a cause of falling.

Yudhishthira left Sahadeva behind and went on with his brothers—and with the dog.

[12–17] When Nakula saw that Draupadi the Dark Lady had fallen, and Pandu's son Sahadeva, he was tormented, for he loved his family, and he himself fell. And when the good-looking Nakula had fallen, Bhima spoke yet again to King Yudhishthira, saying, "This man, my brother, Nakula, never violated dharma and always did what he was asked to do, and he was the handsomest man in the world. But he has fallen on the earth!" The dharmic Yudhishthira, the most intelligent of men, answered Bhima about Nakula: "His view[29] was, 'No one is as handsome as I am; I am the best, the only one.' This thought was rooted in his mind. Nakula has fallen because of that. Come along, Wolf-belly. Everyone inevitably gets whatever is fated for him."

[18–22] But when Pandu's son Arjuna, Driver of White Horses, slayer of enemy heroes, saw that they had fallen, he himself fell after them, burning with grief. And when that unassailable tiger among men, with Indra's brilliance, had fallen and was dying, Bhima said to the king, "I cannot recall anything false in this great-hearted man, even in trivial matters. What caused this corruption[30] that made him fall to the earth?" Yudhishthira said, "Arjuna said, 'I could burn up my enemies in a single day,' boasting of his heroism. But he did not do this, and so he has fallen. Ruddy Arjuna despised all archers, but a man who wishes for greatness must do what he says he will do."

[23–26] The king went on, and then Bhima fell. Fallen, Bhima said to Yudhishthira, the Dharma King, "Look, your majesty! Look down! I, whom you love, have fallen! What made me fall? Tell

---

[29] There is a pun here on *darshana*, "view," which can mean, among other things, "philosophy" (Nakula's opinion that he was gorgeous) or "sight/appearance" (his gorgeousness). Nilakantha says that Nakula fell because of his pride in his beauty.

[30] The word here translated as "corruption," *vikara*, designates a change for the worse in a person's nature or physical or mental condition or morals. The question might also be translated, "Who caused this corruption..."

me, if you know." Yudhishthira said, "You ate too much, and you boast about your vital energy, with no regard for anyone else. That is why, son of Kunti, you have fallen on the ground." Then strong-armed Yudhishthira went on, never looking down. But that one dog followed him—the dog that I have already mentioned to you quite a lot.[31]

Chapter 3: Yudhishthira Goes to Heaven, With a Dog

[1–4] Then Indra came in his chariot to Kunti's son Yudhishthira, making heaven and earth resound everywhere, and said to him, "Get in." But the Dharma King had seen all his brothers fall, and, burning with grief, he said to the Thousand-eyed Indra, "My brothers have fallen here. Let them come with me. Lord of the Gods, I do not want to go to heaven without my brothers.[32] And the delicate princess, who deserves to be happy—let her go with us. Shatterer of Citadels, would you please give your permission for that?"

[5–6] Indra said, "Your brothers and your sons went to heaven before you, and you will see them all, together with the Dark Lady. Do not grieve, Bull of the Bharatas. They threw off their human bodies and went. But you, Bull of the Bharatas, will undoubtedly go to heaven with this body."

[7–8] Yudhishthira said, "Lord of the Past and the Future, this dog has been constantly devoted to me.[33] Let him go with me, for

---

[31] The sudden intrusion of a first-person pronoun representing the narrator is highly unusual. It is as if he anticipates the end of the story and begins to remind the audience that it is, in fact, just a story.

[32] Nilakantha says that the point is that it is better to enjoy good fortune with one's family, not merely by oneself.

[33] Nilakantha says that the burden of the passage that begins here is that one must first share one's happiness with those who are low and close and only enjoy it oneself afterward.

I cannot bear the thought of cruelty." Indra said, "Today, your majesty, you have become immortal, and just like me, and you have won complete glory and great fame, as well as the joys of heaven. Abandon the dog. There is nothing cruel in this."[34]

[9–10] Yudhishthira said, "Noble God of a Thousand Eyes, it is difficult for one who is noble to commit this ignoble act. Don't let me have this glory for which I would have to abandon someone devoted to me." Indra said, "There is no place for dog owners in the world of heaven; for those who are overcome by anger steal the stored-up merits of their sacrificial acts.[35] You should think of that, Dharma King, before you act. Abandon the dog. There is nothing cruel in this."

[11–13] Yudhishthira said, "People have said that abandoning someone devoted to you is a bottomless evil, equal—according to the general opinion—to killing a Brahmin. Therefore, Great Indra, I will never in any way abandon him today just to achieve my own happiness. *Even at the cost of giving up my own life, I would never try to send away someone frightened, devoted, or suffering so much that he said, 'There is nothing else for me,' nor anyone who had come to me for protection, ruined, hoping to save his life. This is my vow, that I would keep forever.*" Indra said, "Those who are overcome by anger carry off what has been offered, sacrificed, or given as an oblation, if it is left uncovered and a dog has looked at it. Therefore, you must abandon this dog, and by abandoning the dog you will win the world of the gods. By abandoning your brothers, and even your

---

[34] Nilakantha glosses Indra's argument as saying that there is no lack of pity involved in rejecting contact with one who is untouchable, *asprishya*.

[35] Nilakantha says that because of the impurity of those who own dogs, there is no place for them in heaven. He also points out that "overpowered by anger" is the name of a group of gods who destroy the fruits of impure offerings. (They are sometimes said to be the descendants of the sage Kashyapa and a daughter of Daksha named "Overpowered by Anger.") But the term may also designate mad dogs, who are notoriously accused of polluting the fruits of sacrifice (merely by looking at the sacrifice) and hence destroying them. (See the Introduction.) The two ideas are combined just two verses later, in 17.3.12, where first the dogs look at the offerings, and then the spirits overpowered by anger destroy them.

darling Dark Lady, Draupadi, you reached this world by your own action.[36] How is it then that you are not abandoning this dog? Now that you have abandoned everything, you have become confused."

[14–15] Yudhishthira said, "There is no such thing as either union or separation[37] between those who are dead and those who will die; this is common knowledge. I could not bring them back to life, and so I abandoned them—but not while they were alive. Handing over someone who has come to you for refuge; killing a woman; taking the property of a Brahmin; and treachery to a friend: these four acts, in my opinion, Indra, are equaled by the act of abandoning someone who is devoted to you."

[16–21] When he heard these words spoken by the Dharma King, the god Dharma took his own form[38] and spoke to King Yudhishthira affectionately, with smooth words of praise: "Your majesty, you are well born, with your father's[39] good conduct and intelligence, and this compassion[40] for all creatures. Once in the past, my son, I tested you in the Dvaita forest, where your brothers were killed when they were trying to get water to drink, and where you abandoned Bhima and Arjuna, your two full brothers, and chose to save the life of Nakula because you wanted the two mothers to be equal.[41] And now, insisting, 'This dog is devoted to me,' you have abandoned[42] the gods' chariot. Because of this, there is no one your equal in heaven. And because of this, Best of the Bharatas, you have

---

[36] Or, perhaps, by your own karma.
[37] The words that he uses to denote "union" and "separation" also mean "alliance "and "breaking an alliance" in the Indian science of politics.
[38] He had been there all along in the form of the dog.
[39] Perhaps Dharma is paying an indirect compliment to himself, Yudhishthira's divine father; he calls Yudhishthira "son" in the very next verse. But Nilakantha is surely right about the primary referent: "You are from a very high family because of your [human] father, Pandu."
[40] Here he uses the positive word for compassion, *anukrosha*, "weeping with."
[41] The story is told at 3.295–299. After he himself had been saved, Yudhishthira then saved Nakula the son of Madri, rather than Arjuna or Bhima (the other two sons of Kunti, Yudhishthira being the third), thus ensuring that each of the two mothers would have a living son, Yudhishthira for Kunti and Nakula for Madri.
[42] The word that Dharma uses here, *tyakta*, which might also be translated "rejected," is the same word that Yudhishthira used when refusing to abandon the dog.

won undying worlds, and you have won the supreme heavenly final destination with your own body."[43]

[22-24] Then Dharma and Indra and the Winds and the two Ashvins[44] and all the other gods and divine sages put Yudhishthira the son of Pandu into the chariot. And all of them went in their own flying palaces, perfected beings that went wherever they wished to go, dustless,[45] virtuous, clean in word, thought, and deed. King Yudhishthira, Scion of the Kuru Family, mounted the chariot and flew swiftly upward, filling heaven and earth with his brilliance.

[25-29] Then Narada, who lived among the gods and knew all about everyone and every world, and who was a great man of *tapas* and a great talker, said, loudly, "The Kuru King has surpassed and eclipsed the fame even of all the royal sages who are in attendance here.[46] For we have never heard of anyone but Yudhishthira the son of Pandu who has won worlds with his own body, filling them with his fame and brilliance and virtue." The dharmic king, hearing Narada's words and not seeing his brothers or the kings who were of his own party, said: "Whether my brothers are in a good place or a bad place today, that is where I want to go. I don't desire any other worlds."

[30-36] When Indra the King of the Gods, Shatterer of Citadels, heard King Yudhishthira's words, devoid of any cruelty, he replied, "Live in this place, which you, an Indra among kings, have won by your own good actions.[47] Why do you still, even today, drag around human

---

[43] The supreme final destination is the ne plus ultra of transmigrational states, or the heavenly transmigrational state beyond which there is nothing. It is not *moksha*; for one thing, Yudhishthira still has his body. Though the Pandavas undergo an intense kind of yoga, their highest goal is simply the highest heaven. What distinguishes Yudhishthira from the others is that he walks into heaven with his own body and only later changes it for a heavenly body.

[44] These five gods are the divine parents of Yudhishthira, Arjuna, Bhima, and Nakula and Sahadeva.

[45] Divine beings cast no shadows, do not sweat or blink or touch the ground with their feet, and are always free of dust.

[46] Nilakantha says they are all together as objects of memory.

[47] Or good karmas.

affection?[48] Joy of the Kurus, you have achieved supreme success, such as no other man has ever achieved; your brothers have *not* achieved such a place. Yet even today, human emotion[49] touches you. This is heaven! Look at the divine sages and perfected beings who live in this triple paradise." But the wise Yudhishthira answered the lordly King of the Gods with this meaningful speech: "I cannot bear to live here without them, Indra, Crusher of Demons. I want to go there where my brothers have gone, and where big, dark Draupadi, has gone, a woman of intelligence, goodness, and virtue, the best of women, the woman I love."[50]

---

[48] "Human affection" can mean either the sorts of affection that humans have or affection for humans. "Drag around" can also have the metaphorical meaning of "ponder" or "reflect upon."

[49] The phrase can mean "human emotion" or "the human condition" or "human nature" or all of the above.

[50] The final phrase could also be translated as "and those I love," but I think this goes against the intended meaning.

Book Eighteen, *Svargarohana Parvan*, The Book of Climbing to Heaven

Preface to Book Eighteen

Book Eighteen might be called "Climbing to Heaven and Falling to Hell," as it deals in some detail with the transfer of karma in hell and its fruition in heaven. Or it might be called, "How to Get to Heaven," as the personae here are already in heaven, and we learn how they got there. This final book expresses several competing views of transmigration, the complex intertwinings of several different heavens, hells, and rebirths, as well as illusory heavens and hells. There are also various ways of imagining translation to heaven: some people join a group, others enter a heavenly form of their own body, still others merge with another body, and so forth. Some humans return to their fathers, others to the gods of whom they are a partial incarnation. Some are given different, heavenly bodies that exactly resemble their old bodies. Yudhishthira is extraordinary in being given the gift of going to heaven in his own body (18.4.2).

The heroes, freed from hell (or from their illusion of hell), go to heaven and to their horror find that their enemies are there too. Their reconciliation to this at first unacceptable fact involves both the relinquishing of their *manyu*, the vengeful pride that had made them cling to their hatred of their enemies, and the revelation that all of them, heroes and villains alike, ultimately become reabsorbed into the gods (or anti-gods) that they were before the story began. In the end, they go on to worlds "beyond which there is nothing," a phrase that evokes the tantalizing via negativa of the Upanishads and leaves us in the dark about the nature of those bright worlds.

Chapter 1: Yudhishthira Reaches Heaven and Encounters Duryodhana

[1-10] When Yudhishthira and the other Pandavas and the allies of Dhritarashtra reached the triple-tiered heaven, Yudhishthira the Dharma King saw Duryodhana seated on a seat, luxuriating in glory, shining like the sun, covered with the signs of heroes, together with the shining gods and the Sadhyas who have done good deeds.[1] Yudhishthira was unable to brook the sight of Duryodhana, and seeing the glory of this "Good" Yodhana,[2] he suddenly turned away, saying loudly, "I do not want these worlds in the company of the greedy and short-sighted Duryodhana. Because of him we destroyed the entire world, and our friends and relations, in a violent battle after we had been tormented, earlier, in the great forest, and our wife Draupadi, the Panchala princess, with her flawless body, she who always did what was dharmic, had been harassed in the midst of the assembly in the presence of the elders.[3] Farewell, gods. I have no desire to gaze upon this 'Good' Yodhana. I want to go where my brothers are."

[11-18] "Not like that," Narada said to him, smiling. "When one lives in heaven, your majesty, even hostility vanishes. Strong-armed Yudhishthira, don't ever talk like that about King Duryodhana.

---

[1] Or who have good karma.

[2] The text has from the start punned on the "good/easy" (*su*) or "evil/difficult" (*dur*) warrior (*yodhana*), calling Duryodhana (whose name means an "evil fighter" or, more positively, a "hard man to fight against") Suyodhana ("a good fighter"). But in this final book, where the moral nature of one's enemy is a central issue, the puns raise more profound questions.

[3] This complaint rehearses the many sufferings of the Pandavas narrated earlier in the *Mahabharata*, beginning in 2.43-72.

Listen to what I am saying. This King Duryodhana is honored along with the thirty gods and with these good, outstanding kings who live in heaven. For he obtained the final destination of the world of heroes when he offered his own body as an oblation in the battle and brought together in battle all of you who are the equals of the gods. This king, who was without fear even in great danger, has won this place through the Kshatriya dharma. My son, you should not hold in your mind what happened because of the dice game, nor should you worry about Draupadi's troubles. And the other troubles that the game of dice caused you, too, in the battles or elsewhere—you should not remember them. Meet with King Duryodhana, as is proper. This is heaven, your majesty. Enmities do not exist here."

[19–26] Then Yudhishthira, the wise Kuru King, asked Narada about his brothers: "If these eternal worlds of heroes[4] belong to the evil Duryodhana, who does not know dharma and was the enemy of his friends on earth, he for whose sake the earth was destroyed, with its horses and chariots and elephants, and we were enflamed by vengeful pride and goaded to take countermeasures against his hostility, then what about my great-hearted brothers, heroes of the world, who undertook great vows and kept their promises and spoke the truth? What worlds do they have now? I want to see them, and Karna, the great-hearted son of Kunti who always kept his promises, and Dhrishtadyumna[5] and Satyaki, and Dhrishtadyumna's sons, princes who went to their death by their weapons, following the Kshatriya dharma. Brahmin, where are these princes? I do not see them, Narada, nor Virata and Drupada, and those who followed Dhrishtaketu. And, Narada, I want to see Shikhandin the Panchala prince and all of Draupadi's sons, and Abhimanyu so hard to conquer."

---

[4] The commentary of Vadiraja here offers this explanation: The worlds of heroes, where heroes who died facing battle enjoy happiness for a little while, are worlds above the ether but below heaven.

[5] Draupadi's brother.

Chapter 2: Yudhishthira Goes to Hell and Meets His Brothers and Draupadi

[1–5] Yudhishthira said, "Wise gods, I do not see here Radha's[6] son Karna, whose power was immeasurable, nor the two great-hearted brothers, Yudhamanyu and Uttamaujas.[7] The great warriors who offered their bodies as oblations in the fire of battle, and the kings and kings' sons who were killed in the battle for my sake—where are all those great warriors who attacked like tigers? Surely those supreme men also won this world? If they and all the great-hearted warriors reached these worlds, I will stay with them. Know this, you gods. But if those kings did not reach this incorruptible and splendid world, I will not live without them and without my relatives and brothers.

[6–12] "For I burn with pain when I hear the words my mother said then, during the funeral ritual: 'Have the libation done for Karna.' And, gods, I burn with grief more and more that I did not follow Karna as soon as I saw that his feet were just like my mother's.[8] For not even Indra could have conquered us in battle if we had had Karna on our side, Karna whose power was incalculable and who could smash enemy armies. And when I failed to recognize Karna, Arjuna the Ambidextrous Archer killed him. Wherever he is, I want to see Karna the son of the Sun, and Bhima of Terrible Attack, dearer to me than my life's breaths, and Arjuna the image of Indra,[9] and the twins who are like the Twins.[10] I want to see Draupadi, the Panchala princess, who always did what was dharmic. I do not want to stay here. I am telling you the truth. Great

---

[6] Radha was the woman of the low Suta caste who adopted Karna.
[7] Two Panchalas killed by Ashvatthaman (10.8.33 and 35).
[8] Yudhishthira expresses, on several occasions, his regret that he did not know that Karna was his older brother; see the Introduction. He has already expressed his regret that he did not realize who Karna was even when he saw the resemblance between Karna's feet and Kunti's feet (12.1.37–42).
[9] Indra is Arjuna's divine father.
[10] That is, Nakula and Sahadeva who are like the twin Ashvins, their fathers; though the compound may also mean, "who are like Yama (god of the dead)."

gods, what use is heaven to me if I do not have my brothers? Where they are is my heaven; I do not regard this as heaven."

[13–21] The gods said, "If you really believe in that place, go there without delay, son. For we will do whatever you want, as Indra the King of the Gods has commanded." Then the gods instructed the messenger of the gods: "Show Yudhishthira his friends." And so Kunti's royal son and the messenger of the gods went together to the place where those bulls among men were. The messenger of the gods went in front, and the king behind him, on a path that was nasty, dangerous, and frequented by evildoers, enveloped in darkness, horrible, reeking with the smells of wrongdoers, with hair for its moss and grass, flesh and blood for its mud, swarming with stinging flies and mosquitoes and lice and fleas, surrounded by corpses on all sides, on this side and that, strewn with bones and hair, full of worms and maggots, encircled on all sides by a blazing fire, overrun by crows and owls and vultures with iron beaks, crowded with ghosts the size of the Vindhya mountains but with mouths like needles,[11] strewn here and there with severed arms, thighs, and hands covered in fat and blood, and entrails and amputated legs.

[22–25] The dharmic king, pondering a great deal, walked down the middle of that dangerous, hair-raising path that stank with the stench of corpses. He saw a river full of boiling hot water, very dangerous to ford,[12] and a forest where the leaves were swords, the ground covered with sharp razors. Heated mud and sand, free-standing iron rocks, and iron pots of simmering sesame oil were all around. Kunti's son Yudhishthira also saw spikey silk-cotton trees[13] with sharp thorns, painful to touch, and he saw the tortures of the evildoers.

---

[11] These are the hungry ghosts with great bellies and tiny mouths, never satisfied.

[12] This is the Vaitarani River of hell, that was foreshadowed in the description of doomed Dvaraka in Chapter 6 of Book 16.

[13] The *shalmalika* tree (*seemul*, Bombax malabaricum) has red flowers and very long, sharp thorns, which were used for torture. It is said that even monkeys cannot climb it.

[26–30] When he noticed the vile stench, he said to the messenger of the gods, "How far must we go on such a road? And where are my brothers? You should tell me that. And to which of the gods does this place belong? I want to know that." When the messenger of the gods heard what the Dharma King said, he stopped and said to him, "This is as far as I go. For I must turn back; that is what those who dwell in heaven told me. If you are tired, your majesty, then you should come along with me." Disgusted and fainting from that smell, Yudhishthira decided to turn back, and he turned around.

[31–35]. But when the dharmic king had turned back, filled with grief and sorrow, he heard there the wretched voices of people speaking all around him: "Hello!" "Over here!" "Son of Dharma!" "Royal Sage!" "Virtuous, noble Pandava!" "Stop as a favor to us, just for a short moment. When you come near, you who are hard to conquer, a pleasant breeze blows, bringing your sweet fragrance, which gives us comfort, dear old friend.[14] We will get relief for a long time by looking at you, son of Kunti, bull among men, best of kings. Stay, even for a moment, strong-armed Heir of Kuru. While you stay here, the torture does not pain us."

[36–41] He heard many pitiful voices like that in that place, from people who were suffering, crying out on all sides. And hearing those words from people who spoke of their misery, Yudhishthira felt pity for them and said, "Oh! What suffering!" and stayed there. The Pandava had heard those voices before, again and again, long ago, but he did not recognize them as they came from those wasted, suffering people. Not realizing whose voices they were, Yudhishthira the son of Dharma said, "Who are you, good sirs, and why are you staying here?" Then they all spoke out all around him, "I am Karna." "I am Bhima." "I am Arjuna." "Nakula." "I am

---

[14] Slipped in among all the grandiose royal epithets is the word "*tata*," a term of affection and intimacy usually used to address a person much older or younger, like "grandpa" or "sonny."

Sahadeva." "I am Dhrishtadyumna." "Draupadi." "Draupadi's sons." They cried out like that.

[42–49] When the king heard these voices, fit for that place, he wondered, "Is this the work of fate? What foul deed did these great-hearted people commit[15]—Karna, or Draupadi the slender-waisted Panchala princess, or Draupadi's sons? I don't know of anything bad that the people who are now in this evil-smelling, terrible place did, for all of them did good deeds.[16] And what did the evil king, 'Good' Yodhana, Dhritarashtra's son, do so that he enjoys such glory, along with all his foot-followers? He sits like great Indra with Lakshmi,[17] receiving the highest honor. What caused this corruption[18] that made these others now go to hell? They know all dharmas, and they are heroes, most intent upon the sacred texts and truth, dedicated to the Kshatriya dharma, wise sacrificers, generous with gifts to priests. Am I asleep and dreaming, even while I am awake? I keep trying to figure it out, but I can't figure it out. Damn! Has my mind been corrupted, or deluded?" King Yudhishthira pondered like this in various ways, full of grief and sorrow, his senses bewildered by doubt.

[50–54] Then King Yudhishthira vented his sharp anger. The son of Dharma reviled the gods and even Dharma. Scalded by the sharp smell, he said to the messenger of the gods: "Go, good sir, to those whose messenger you are. I will not go there; I am staying. Tell them that, messenger. For contact with me brings comfort to these my brothers here." The messenger went from the wise son of Pandu to where Indra the King of the Gods, the God of a Hundred Sacrifices, sat. He reported what Yudhishthira the Dharma King wished to do, all of it, just as the son of Dharma had said it.

---

[15] Or, perhaps, "What terrible karma did they amass?"
[16] Or, perhaps, "for all of them had good karma."
[17] The goddess of good fortune, often regarded as the wife of kings.
[18] In 17.2.20, Bhima used this phrase, and in particular the word for "corruption," *vikara*, to question the moral change that made Arjuna fail to climb to heaven. And again, the question might also be translated, "Who caused this corruption . . ."

Chapter 3: Yudhishthira Remains in Heaven and Bathes in the Heavenly Ganges

[1–8] While Kunti's son, Yudhishthira the Dharma King, remained there for a moment, the gods arrived with Indra at their head. And Dharma himself came to King Yudhishthira, the Kuru King, taking on a body in order to test the king. When the assembled gods, worthy in their births and deeds, had arrived there, with their luminous bodies, that darkness disappeared.[19] The tortures of evildoers were not seen there, nor the Crossing-Over River, with its spikey silk-cotton trees. The frightful iron pots and rocks were not seen, and the mutilated bodies that Kunti's son King Yudhishthira had seen there all around had become invisible. Then a gentle wind blew in the presence of the gods, very cool, pleasant on the skin, carrying a fragrant scent. The Maruts with Indra, and the Vasus and Ashvins, and the Sadhyas, and Rudras and Adityas, and the others who dwell in heaven, and the perfected beings and supreme sages—they all came there where King Yudhishthira, the brilliant son of Dharma, was standing.

[9–15] Then Indra, the Lord of the Gods, cloaked in supreme glory, spoke to Yudhishthira, beginning with words of conciliation: "Strong-armed Yudhishthira, all the gods are pleased with you. Come, come. You have done so much, your majesty, tiger among men. You have achieved success, your majesty, and won undying worlds. *And the permanent ultimate destination of your brothers and friends is most honorable.* Don't give way to vengeful pride; listen to what I have to say.[20] My dear son, all kings must inevitably see hell. Bull among men, there are two collections, one of good and one of evil. Whoever enjoys his good deeds first (in heaven) goes afterward to hell. And whoever experiences hell first goes afterward to

---

[19] See the Introduction for a discussion of this verse, as well as this whole episode, by the commentators Nilakantha and Vadiraja.
[20] Nilakantha says that this dispels Yudhishthira's vengeful pride at the thought of his enemies in heaven and his sadness at the thought of his brothers in hell.

heaven. *Someone who has mostly good karma experiences hell first. Unfallen one, you have mostly good karma and just a small amount of crooked karma.* A person who has mostly bad karma experiences heaven first; therefore I made you go this way, your majesty, because I wished to do what was best for you. For you crushed Drona with a deception about his son, and so, your majesty, you were made to see hell just in the form of a deception.[21] And just like you, so too Bhima, and Kunti's son Arjuna and the Twins, and Draupadi the Dark Lady went to hell just in the form of a deception.

[16–19] "Come, tiger among men; they have been freed from their faults, and the people on your side, princes killed in battle for you, bull among men, have all reached heaven. Look at them! And Karna, for whose sake you are suffering, the great archer, best of all who bear arms, has achieved supreme success. Look at Karna, your majesty, the son of the Sun, a tiger among men, established in his own place. Let go of your grief, strong-armed bull among men. And see your brothers and the other princes on your side, each of whom has reached his own place. Let this fever in your mind disappear.

[20–27] "At first you experienced misery, but from now on, Kaurava, enjoy yourself here with me, never ill, no longer grieving. My dear son, strong-armed Pandava, enjoy the fruit of the good karma that you yourself won by your *tapas*, and by the gifts you gave. Let the divine Gandharvas and the heavenly Apsarases, in their dustless garments, serve you in comfort today in heaven. Enjoy the worlds that your consecration won and your horse sacrifice augmented, as well as the great fruit of your *tapas*. For, great-armed Yudhishthira, son of Kunti, your worlds in which you will enjoy yourself are far above those of the kings, equal to those of Harishchandra.[22] Where Mandhatri is, and the royal sage King Bhagiratha, and Bharata the son of Duhshanta, there you will enjoy

---

[21] See the Introduction for the story of the half-lie that Yudhishthira told to Drona.
[22] Harishchandra was a king who sacrificed everything to win the right to enter heaven with his body.

yourself. Here, your majesty, son of Kunti, is the Ganges in the sky, the sacred river of the gods, which purifies the triple world. After you dive into it, your majesty, you will be at rest. And when you have bathed in it, your human nature will leave you. You will have no more grief, no weariness, and you will let go of your hatred."

[28–33] When the King of the Gods had said this to Yudhishthira, King of the Kauravas, Dharma, who had taken on a visible body, said to his own son: "Greetings, your majesty. I am pleased with you, my very wise little son, because you are devoted to me, and you speak the truth, and you have forbearance and self-control. This was the third time I tested you, your majesty, son of Kunti, but nothing, no matter the cause, can make you waver from your own nature. First you were tested in that matter of the firesticks in the Dvaita forest, and you passed that test.[23] And when your brothers were dead, and Draupadi, I tested you there again, my son, taking on the form of a dog.[24] This was the third test, and since you wish to remain for the sake of your brothers, you who are so fortunate, you have been purified and can relax, for all your stains have vanished.

[34–37] "Nor are your brothers staying in hell, your majesty, son of Kunti; this was an illusion staged by Great Indra, King of the Gods. Inevitably all kings must see hell, my dear boy.[25] Therefore you experienced this supreme misery, but just for a moment. Nor does Arjuna the Ambidextrous Archer deserve hell for a long time, your majesty, nor Bhima, nor the Twins who are bulls among men, nor Karna, the hero who speaks the truth. Nor does the Dark Princess Draupadi deserve hell, Yudhishthira. Come, come, Best of the Bharatas. See the Ganges that flows through the three worlds."

---

[23] The story (which begins when a Brahmin's firesticks become entangled in a deer's antlers—it's a long story) is told at 3.295-299, and Dharma mentions it at 17.3.19. The test consisted first of a series of metaphysical riddles that Yudhishthira solved correctly, and then in his choice of a son of Madri to survive, along with himself.
[24] This test is narrated at 17.3.7-20.
[25] This is exactly what Indra had said to Yudhishthira twenty verses earlier. Indra says, My dear son, all kings must inevitably see hell, in verse 11 above, in this very chapter.

[38–41] Then the royal sage Yudhishthira went with Dharma and with all those who dwell among the thirty gods. Plunging into the Ganges, the purifying, sacred river of the gods that the sages praise, the king abandoned his human body. Submerged in that water, free of hatred, all his suffering over, Yudhishthira the Dharma King assumed a heavenly body. And then the wise Yudhishthira, the Kuru King, went with Dharma, surrounded by the gods and praised by the great sages,[26] *to the place where the heroic tigers among men, descendants of Pandu and descendants of Dhritarashtra, were enjoying themselves, in their own places, for their vengeful pride was gone.*

Chapter 4: Yudhishthira in Heaven Meets the Reborn Warriors from Both Sides

[1–8] Then King Yudhishthira, honored by the gods with the sages and the hosts of the Maruts, went where the bulls of the Kurus were. There he saw Krishna, the Finder of Cows, who now had a sacred[27] body, shining from within his own form;[28] he could be recognized by the resemblance to the very body that had been seen before. With him were the heavenly weapons, both horrible and divine, the discus and so forth, that now had the bodies of men. And he was attended by the Ruddy Arjuna, who cast a beautiful light. Then, in another place, Yudhishthira the Joy of the Kurus saw Karna, best of those who bear arms, with the twelve Adityas.[29] And then, in yet another place, he saw Bhima, with that very body, surrounded

---

[26] Nilakantha says that he went to the place where the Pandavas were, with the gods.
[27] The word *brahmya*, here translated as "sacred," may designate a body made of either the Veda or ultimate reality, *brahman*. Nilakantha says it means a body to be propitiated by Brahmans or even by the god Brahma.
[28] I.e., with no external source of light.
[29] As Karna is the son of the Sun, it is appropriate for him to be with the Adityas, sun gods.

by the host of the Maruts.[30] Yudhishthira the Joy of the Kurus saw Nakula and Sahadeva, blazing with their own brilliance, at the place of the Ashvins. And he saw Draupadi, the Panchala princess, garlanded with white lotuses and blue lotuses, standing there with the splendor of the sun, for she had reached heaven with her body.[31] *Seeing that she had a heavenly body and was adorned with heavenly ornaments, Indra the Lord of Power spoke to Yudhishthira the Dharma King.* King Yudhishthira wanted to question her immediately, but the lord Indra, King of the Gods, told him this story:

[9-13] "This is Shri, who became a human being in the form of Draupadi for your sake. She was born of no womb, Yudhishthira, but is the sweet-smelling darling of the people. Born in the family of Drupada, she lived with and served you and your brothers, for the god Shiva Who Holds a Trident in His Hand made her for the pleasure of all of you.[32] These five illustrious Gandharvas, your majesty, who shine like fires and have immeasurable power, are the sons of Draupadi and the five of you. Behold the king of the Gandharvas, and recognize that he is the wise Dhritarashtra, your father's older brother. And this man, shining like fire, is your older brother, Karna, fathered by the Sun, Kunti's first and best son, though he was known as Radha's son. He is going with the Adityas; look at him, bull among men.

[14-19] "See, your majesty, the Vrishnis and Andhakas, great warriors, and Satyaki and the other men, and the Bhojas, great warriors, among the hosts of the Sadhyas, gods, Vasus, and Maruts.

---

[30] As Bhima is the son of the wind (Vayu), he is with the Maruts, wind gods. "That very body" seems to mean that Bhima has a heavenly body identical with his human body, though immortal.

[31] This seems to contradict Narada's statement (at 17.3.27) that Yudhishthira was the only one who got to heaven with his body. But Draupadi does not really count as a *human* who gets to heaven with her body because, unlike the Pandavas, she had a supernatural birth (see the Introduction). She goes to heaven with her husbands, like an ordinary woman, but then she merges with Fire (from whom she had been born) because she was an incarnation of the goddess Shri, as Yudhishthira is about to be informed.

[32] See the Introduction for the story of how Draupadi in a former life asked Shiva five times for a husband.

154   THE LAST BOOKS OF THE *MAHABHARATA*

See, in the company of Soma, Abhimanyu the son of Subhadra, the great archer unconquered by any enemy, with a luster like that of the moon. This is Pandu, your father, a great archer, united with Kunti and Madri and approaching me on a heavenly chariot. See, your majesty, King Bhishma, Shantanu's son, with the Vasus, and observe Drona, your teacher, at Brihaspati's side. And here, Pandava, are other kings who were your fighters, going along together with the Gandharvas and the Yakshas and the Punyajanas. Some special men achieved the final destination of Guhyakas; when they abandoned their bodies, they won heaven by their good thoughts, words, and deeds."

Chapter 5: Everyone Becomes the Gods They Always Were

In the opening verses of this chapter, Janamejaya, the king in the frame, asks about the final destinations: "How long did the Pandavas remain in heaven? Or did they perhaps have a place there that would last forever? Or, at the end of their karma, what final destination did they reach?" The rest of the chapter sidesteps rather than answers the king's questions.

[7–8] All people must go from heaven at the end of their karmas. Listen to this secret of the gods, that was told by the brilliant, fiery ancient sage with the divine gaze, Vyasa the son of Parashara, who had undertaken great vows, whose understanding cannot be fathomed, who knows everything, who knows the final destinations of all karmas.

[9–15] Bhishma, with his great brilliance and great splendor, reached the Vasus, for precisely eight Vasus are visible.[33] Drona,

---

[33] Bhishma was one of the eight Vasus, bright gods in the sky. While he was temporarily exiled to earth as the son of Santanu, there were only seven Vasus left in the sky; now that he has returned to heaven, eight Vasus are visible there again (1.91–94). See also 15.39.15.

the best of the Angirases, entered Brihaspati, and Kritavarman, the son of Hridika, entered the troop of the Maruts. Pradyumna entered Sanatkumara, whence he had come, and Dhritarashtra reached the worlds of Kubera the Lord of Wealth, which are hard to get. The glorious Gandhari with Dhritarashtra, and Pandu with his two wives, went to the palace of Great Indra. Virata and Drupada, Prince Dhrishtaketu, and Nishatha and Akrura and Samba, Bhanu, Kampa, and Viduratha, Bhurishravas, Shala, and King Bhuri, and Ugrasena and Kamsa and the heroic Vasudeva, and Uttara, the bull among men, with his brother Shanka—these excellent men entered the All-Gods.

[16–20] Varchas, the son of Soma, with his great brilliance and splendor, had become Abhimanyu the son of Ruddy Arjuna, lion among men. When he had fought according to the Kshatriya dharma, as no other man had ever done, at the end of his karma this dharmic warrior entered Soma. Karna entered the Sun, his father. Shakuni reached Dvapara,[34] and Dhrishtadyumna reached Fire.[35] All of Dhritarashtra's sons had been Yatudhanas, evil spirits puffed up with power; now purified by weapons, great-hearted and prosperous, they went to heaven. And King Yudhishthira and Vidura, the son of a servant woman, entered Dharma himself.[36] The lord god called the Infinite[37] entered the watery world under the earth, for he supported the earth with his yoga, as the Grandfather[38] had arranged. *Balarama with his great brilliance was also the serpent Shesha, a Naga. Krishna, the son of Vasudeva, a portion of Vishnu,*

---

[34] Dvapara is the god of the Deuce, the third (and second to the worst) throw of the dice and the third (and second to the worst) of the four Yugas, the age in which the *Mahabharata* is set. (See Introduction). Dvapara had become incarnate as Shakuni (15.39.10), who played dice on behalf of Duryodhana and cheated Yudhishthira of his kingdom.
[35] Fire is the divine father of Dhrishtadyumna (and of his sister Draupadi).
[36] Dharma had become incarnate as Vidura and was the divine father of Yudhishthira. See 15.33 for the death of Vidura.
[37] The serpent Shesha is called Ananta, "The Infinite." Balarama's re-entry into Shesha is narrated at 16.5.11–15.
[38] The Creator.

at the end of his karma entered Vishnu, the eternal god of gods, called Narayana. *In order to do a favor for the universe, the guru of the universe, the son of Vasudeva, ascended to heaven with a divine form and disappeared.*

[21–24] The sixteen thousand wives who were the harem of Krishna the son of Vasudeva plunged into the Sarasvati; in the course of Time, they became Apsarases and joined the son of Vasudeva. *Abandoning their bodies there, they climbed back into heaven.* The great warriors who had been killed in that great battle, Ghatotkacha and the others, all assumed the form of gods and Yakshas. Duryodhana's allies were well known to be Rakshasas, but by degrees they reached all the worlds beyond which there is nothing. Those bulls among men entered the palace of Great Indra and the wise Kubera and the worlds of Varuna.[39]

[25] Now this entire adventure of the Kurus and the Pandavas has been narrated for you in full detail.

Epilogue: The Fruits of Hearing the *Mahabharata*

Preface to the Epilogue

Much of what is in this final panegyric of the text is also found near the very start of the *Mahabharata* (at 1.56.12–33). The opening five verses of this section are omitted here because they narrate Janamejaya's reception of the story, in the frame.

The four verses near the end (18.5.47–50) are called the Savitri of the *Mahabharata*, which is to say the *Mahabharata*'s equivalent of the three-verse passage of the Vedas called the Savitri hymn (*Rig Veda* 3.62.10–12), also known as the Gayatri, the most sacred

---

[39] The commentator Vadiraja says that the men are Virata, Drupada, Bhishma, Drona, and so forth, or else they are the children of Dhritarashtra; they had all been Yatudhanas puffed up with pride. For, he continues, the princes who were the allies of Duryodhana have not been mentioned; they entered Danavas, Guhyakas, and Gandharvas.

prayer in Hinduism, which should be recited every day at dawn. This passage asserts that these four verses of the *Mahabharata* have the same sacred force as that Vedic passage and are, in that sense, the Savitri of this text. It also implies that, by the principle of equivalence that often operates in Sanskrit texts, these four verses are the equivalent of the whole *Mahabharata*: reading them gives the same benefits as reading the whole text. The verb *path*, used throughout this final passage and translated here as "recite," indicates reading from a written text or reciting from memory.

[31–34] This auspicious narrative, called a history, is the supreme purifier. It was given a set form by the Dark Sage Vyasa, who always told the truth, who was omniscient and knew about fate[40] and knew dharma, who had extrasensory perception,[41] who was pure and had a soul realized by *tapas*, who exercised lordship, knew Sankhya[42] and yoga, had an intelligence with more than one line of thought and saw with a divine gaze. He spread in the world the fame of the great-hearted Pandavas and the other Kshatriyas who had prodigious brilliance and wealth. *And [he told about] the sport of Krishna the son of Vasudeva, the god of gods with the bow of horn, and the absorption into [human] birth of all the portions of the gods.*

[35–36] The wise man who always proclaims this constantly at every lunar fortnight[43] wins heaven and goes to the world of *brahman*, for his evils are shaken off. *When someone listens, attentively, to this Veda of Vyasa the Dark Sage, the evil caused by killing a Brahmin vanishes at that very moment.* And whoever recites at least a quarter of a verse of it to Brahmins, at a ritual for the ancestors, procures inexhaustible food and drink for his ancestors. *Anyone who hears this worthy history will achieve a good reward. It should*

---

[40] The word *vidhi* can mean "ritual" or "method" as well as "fate," but the context makes "fate" the most relevant meaning.
[41] *Atindriya*, literally "beyond" (*ati*) "the senses" (*indriya*).
[42] An important ancient Indian philosophy.
[43] This phrase can also mean, "book by book."

be heard by a woman with no son and also by a pregnant woman; she will give birth to a heroic son or to a daughter who will marry a king.

[37] Whatever sin a person commits by day in his senses or even in his heart, he is freed from at that sunset by narrating the Mahabharata. Whatever evil a Brahmin commits with his senses at night, he is freed from at dawn by narrating the Mahabharata. It is called the Mahabharata *because it tells of the great birth (mahajjanma) of the Bharatas. Whoever knows its exegesis is freed from all evils. The* [Maha]Bharata *is the eighteen Puranas,*[44] *all the dharma texts, and the Vedas and their supplementary texts, all standing together in one place, in one body. Let this lion's roar of the great-hearted sage, the maker of the eighteen Puranas and of the great ocean of the Vedas, be heard.*

Long ago, the lord, the sage, the Dark Lord of the Island, made this whole great Bharata *in three years. A man who studies it just once obtains even the reward that comes from reading the four Vedas three times. Brahmin-killing and the other evils disappear for the one who hears it. The good woman who longs for the happiness of offspring, and who listens constantly to this history, brings forth a heroic son and a daughter who will marry a king; there should be no doubt about this. Prosperity, fame, and knowledge are always with the one who gives ear, with devotion, to this* Mahabharata *that is called Victory.*

[38–40] Whatever there is here about dharma, politics, pleasure, and freedom,[45] you can also find elsewhere but what is not here is nowhere. *Where the great* Bharata *that is called Victory is constantly recited, prosperity, fame, and knowledge always rejoice, and sons and grandsons and all good things increase. The gods, perfected beings, and supreme sages, ecstatic, honor the one who speaks, hears, or writes the* Bharata. *Men who do not give honor here to the person*

---

[44] The Puranas are later Sanskrit texts devoted to stories about and rituals for the Hindu gods.

[45] These are the four goals of life, the *purusharthas*: dharma, *artha*, *kama*, and *moksha*. In the body of the *Mahabharata*, they are usually listened just as a triad, omitting *moksha*.

who speaks the Mahabharata suffer the destruction of all their rituals, and the gods curse them. This history, called "Victory," should be heard by anyone who wants power, by a king and by the king's sons and also by a pregnant woman. *An intelligent believer [astika] filled with faith rejoices when he hears this and obtains what he desires more than anything else. Hearing it even once destroys Brahminicide; hearing it twice, with devotion, one obtains the fruits of a horse sacrifice. By hearing it, or reading it, three times, with devotion, one achieves the auspicious final destination of brahman, never to return again. In the house of the man who honors the recitation of the Mahabharata, the gods dwell, and the god Narayana himself, the lotus-eyed Krishna son of Vasudeva, dwells there.* A person who desires heaven will get heaven, and one who desires victory will get victory. A pregnant woman gets a son or a well-married daughter.

[41–42] The Dark Lord of the Island, in his desire for dharma, wove together the yet unknown tale of the Bharatas in three years. *He made a collection of 6,000,000 stanzas. 3,000,000 stanzas are kept in the world of the gods; 1,500,000 should be known to be in the world of the ancestors, and 1,400,000 in the world of Nagas and Yakshas. 100,000 were expounded among men.* Narada told it to the gods, and Asita Devala[46] told it to the ancestors. Shuka[47] told it to the Rakshasas and Yakshas, and Vaisampayana[48] told it to mortals.

[43–45] This worthy history has great meaning and value and is equal to the Veda; whoever has it recited to the three classes,[49] putting the Brahmins first, that man will become free from evil, achieve fame here on earth, and reach supreme success; I have no doubt about this. *His soul is purified of all evils, his mind is set upon purity, and he obtains fame and enjoys great happiness here. By Vyasa's favor*

---

[46] Asita Devala was a great sage, author of Vedic hymns.
[47] Shuka is Vyasa's son. The word *shuka* means "parrot," an appropriate name for a bard who recites a memorized text.
[48] Vaisampayana is the bard narrating the received text, translated in this book, to King Janamejaya, in the frame.
[49] That is, the first three of the four classes, the triad of the "twice-born," excluding the Shudras.

he also goes to the world of heaven. A Brahmin who knows all of this knows the meaning and essence of all the Vedas, and he is to be constantly given honor and respect. When [the recitation of] this Book of Climbing to Heaven is completed, one should honor the Brahmin who recited it and make him happy by giving him clothes. If a man of faith studies even a quarter of a verse of this worthy recitation of the Bharatas, he is purified of all his evils, without exception.

[46–50] Long ago, the great sage, the lord Vyasa, made this collection and taught it to his son Shuka, along with these four verses:

Thousands of mothers and fathers, and hundreds of sons and wives, have experienced transmigrations and gone on, and others will go on.

Thousands of states of joy, and hundreds of states of fear, enter the fool every day, but not the learned man.

I myself cry out with my arms up,[50] but no one hears me. From dharma comes politics and also pleasure;[51] why is it not practiced?

A man should never abandon dharma out of desire or fear or greed, not even for the sake of his life. Dharma is eternal, but happiness and unhappiness are transient; the soul is eternal, but its cause is transient.[52]

[51–54] Whoever gets up at dawn and recites this *Savitri* hymn of the *Bharata* obtains the fruit of the *Bharata* and comprehends the supreme *brahman*. Both the venerable ocean and the mountain Himalaya are famous as treasure troves of jewels, and the *Bharata* is said to be just like that. Whoever recites the story of the *Mahabharata*, with his mind well collected, achieves

---

[50] At 15.45.41 raised arms are a sign of intense grief.
[51] He speaks of dharma, artha, and kama, three of the four goals of a human life, and not, significantly, of *moksha*, the fourth goal that was added later.
[52] The word "cause" (*hetu*) might also mean "reason" or "occasion," i.e., the circumstances under which the soul becomes incarnate.

supreme success; I have no doubt about this. Whoever thoroughly understands, as it is being spoken, the *Bharata* that slipped out of the cup of the lips of Vyasa of the Island and is immeasurable, worthy, purifying, auspicious, and removes all evils—what use has he for ablutions with the waters of Lake Pushkara?[53]

This completes the revered *Mahabharata*.

---

[53] Lake Pushkara is a holy pilgrimage site in Rajasthan.

Appendices

Appendix 1: Adjectives Applied to Several Characters

Achala, immovable
Achyuta, unfallen
Amala, spotless
Amitabuddhi, of immeasurable intelligence
Amitatejas, of immeasurable brilliance
Anagha, faultless
Anindita, blameless
Apratima, unparalleled
Arindama, subduer of enemies, king
Atmavan, self-possessed
Balavant, Balin, powerful
Balinam Shrestha, best of the powerful
Bharata (with a long "a" in the first syllable), any descendant of King Bharata
Brahmarshi, Brahmin sage
Devarshi, divine sage
Devi, queen
Dharmacharin, acting with dharma, dharmic
Dharmajna, knowing dharma, dharmic
Dharmashila, having a dharmic nature, dharmic
Dharmatman, having the soul of dharma, dharmic
Dharmya, dharmic
Dhiman, wise
Dvija, twice-born, a Brahmin
Dvijamukhya, chief of the twice-born
Dvijasattama, best of the twice-born
Dyutiman, shining
Janadhipa, overlord of the people, king
Janeshvara, lord of the people, king
Kaurava, Kauravya, descendant or heir of Kuru
Kshattri, a servant, son of a Kshatriya father and Shudra mother
Kshitipati, lord of the earth, king
Kurunandana, joy of the Kurus
Kurupati, lord of the Kurus

Kurupungava, bull of the Kurus
Lokapujita, honored throughout the world
Mahabahu, strong-armed
Mahabhaga, fortunate, privileged, lucky, eminent
Mahabhuj, greatly enjoying
Mahabuddhi, with great intelligence, highly intelligent
Mahadyuti, with great luster
Mahamanas, high-minded, very wise
Mahamati, high-minded, very wise
Mahamuni, great sage
Mahaprajna, very wise
Maharaja, great king
Maharatha, having great chariots, a great warrior
Mahatapas, having great *tapas*, great in his *tapas*
Mahatejas, of great brilliance, brilliant
Mahatman, great-hearted
Mahavira, with great manly energy
Mahayogi, with great powers of yoga
Mahipala, protector of the earth, king
Mahipati, lord of the earth, king
Manishin, wise
Manushardula, tiger among men
Medhavin, intelligent
Munipungava, bull of sages
Naradhipa, overlord of men, king
Narapati, protector of men, king
Nararshabha, bull among men
Naravyaghra, tiger among men
Nripa, protector of men, king
Nripasattama, best of the protectors of men
Nripati, protector of men, king
Nrisimha, lion among men
Pandava, descendant of Pandu
Parama, supreme
Paramadharmika, most dharmic
Paramarshi, supreme sage
Parantapa, heater of foes
Paravirahan, killer of enemies
Parthiva, ruler of the earth, king
Parthivarshabha, bull among kings
Paurava, descendant of Puru
Prabhu, ruler, king
Prithivipala, protector of the earth, king
Prithivipati, lord of the earth, king

Pungava, bull
Punya, meritorious
Purusharshabha, bull among men
Purushavyaghra, tiger among men
Purushottama, Purushasattama, supreme man
Raja, king
Rajaputra, son of a king, prince
Rajarshi, royal sage
Rajashardula, tiger among kings
Rajendra, lord of kings, king
Rishiputra, son of a sage
Sadhu/Sadhvi, good man/woman
Shobana, magnificent
Shrestha, the best
Shubha, glorious
Shriman, glorious
Sumahamanas, with a very great mind
Sumahatman, with a very great soul
Tapasvin, possessing *tapas*
Tapodhana, rich in *tapas*
Tejasvin, brilliant
Vadatam vara, best of those who talk
Varangara, good woman
Vashin, powerful
Vibhu, lord, king
Vidvan, learned
Vipra, inspired; a Brahmin
Vira, hero
Viryavan, heroic
Visham pate, ruler of the people, king
Vishishtama, most distinguished
Yashasvin, splendid
Yoshitam vara, best of women
Yudham pati, lord of warriors

Appendix 2: Names and Epithets of Central Characters

Abhimanyu, son of Arjuna and Subhadra, husband of Uttara and father of Parikshit
  Pandavadayada, Heir of the Pandava (patronymic)
  Saubhadra, Son of Subhadra (matronymic)

Agni, god of fire
  Saptarshi, God with Seven Rays
Arjuna, son of Pandu and Kunti (and the god Indra)
  Bharata, Descendant of King Bharata
  Bharatarshabha, Bull of the Bharatas
  Bibhatsu, Disdainful, loathing, feeling disgust
  Dhananjaya, Wealth-winning
  Jaya, Victory
  Jishnu, Victorious
  Kauravya, Heir of Kuru
  Kuruvyagra, Tiger of the Kurus
  Nara, "Man," companion of Krishna as Narayana
  Pakashasani, Son of Indra the Chastiser of [the demon] Paka
  Pandava, Son of Pandu
  Pandavanandana, Joy of the Pandus
  Partha, Son of Pritha/Kunti (matronymic designating any of the sons of Kunti, but usually referring to Arjuna)
  Phalguna, Ruddy
  Savyasachin, the Ambidextrous (literally the left-handed, more precisely, the *also* left-handed) Archer
  Shakrabija, the Seed of Shakra (Indra)
  Shvetashva, Driver of White Horses
  Vijaya, Victory
Ashvatthaman, son of Drona
  Drauni, Son of Drona
Ashvins, twin equine gods, fathers of Nakula and Sahadeva, by Madri
  Yamajau, Sons of Yama
Balarama, older brother of Krishna
  Halayudha, with the Plough as his Weapon
  Rama
Bharata, the founding king of the dynasty
  [with a long "a" in the first syllable] any descendant of that king
Bhima, second oldest son of Pandu and Kunti (and son of the Wind god)
  Bhimakarman, of Fearful Deeds
  Bhimasena, Leader of a Fearful Army
  Marutatmaja, Son of the Wind
  Vrikodara, Wolf-belly (because he was a great eater)
Bhishma, son of Shantanu and the river Ganges
  Gangeya, Son of Ganges
  Shantavana, Son of Shantanu
Brihaspati, chief minister of Indra, king of the gods
Daruka, Krishna's charioteer
Dhritarashtra, the blind Kuru king, son of Vichitravirya, father of Duryodhana
  Kauravavamshabhrit, Upholder of the Dynasty of Descendants of Kuru

Kauravanandana, Joy of the Descendants of Kuru
Kauravarshabha, Bull of the Descendants of Kuru
Kauravavamshabhrit, Pillar of the Kaurava Dynasty
Kauravendra, Lord of the Descendants of Kuru
Kauravya, Descendant of Kuru
Kurudvaha, Scion of the Kurus
Kururaja, King of the Kurus
Kurushrestha, Best of the Kurus
Vaichitravirya, Son of Vichitravirya
Draupadi, wife of all five Pandavas
   Krishna, the Dark Lady
   Panchali, the Pancala Princess/Woman
   Yajnasena, Daughter of Drupada (who was called Yajnasena, "Army of Sacrifice")
Gandhari, wife of Dhritarashtra, mother of the Kauravas
Ganges, the river, often incarnate as a goddess
   Bhagirathi, [brought to earth by king] Bhagiratha,
   Jahnavi, Daughter of King Jahnu
   Trilokaga, Going in the Three Worlds (heaven, earth, and the underworld)
   Tripathaga, Going on Three Paths
Hastinapur, the City named after an Elephant
   Gajasahvika, Named after an Elephant
   Varanahvayam, Named after an Elephant
Indra, king of the gods, god of the storm
   Acyuta, Unfallen
   Balahantri, Slayer of the Demon Bala (or Destroyer of Power)
   Daityanibarhana, Crusher of Demons
   Devaraja, King of the Gods
   Ishvara, the Lord
   Mahendra, Great Indra
   Marudgana, Leader of the Host of the Winds
   Pakashasana, Chastiser of [the demon] Paka
   Purandhara, Shatterer of Citadels,
   Puruhuta, Invoked by Many
   Sahasraksha, Thousand-eyed
   Shachipati, Shachi's Husband or Husband of Power
   Shakra, Powerful
   Shatakratu, the God of a Hundred Sacrifices; a pun, a god to whom 100 [horse] sacrifices have been made and a king [of the gods] who made 100 [horse] sacrifices
   Vajradhara, Bearer of the Thunderbolt
   Vasava, Chief of the Vasus
Indraprastha, the Plain of Indra, capital of the Bharata dynasty

168   APPENDICES

Janamejaya (Causing Men to Tremble), a king to whom the *Mahabharata* is narrated, son of Parikshit
Kali, the fourth and worst of the four Ages
Karna, son of Kunti and the Sun, adopted son of a bard/charioteer and Radha
    Radheya, Radha's son
    Suryaputra, Son of the Sun
    Sutaputra, Son of a Bard/Charioteer
Krishna, son of Vasudeva, sometimes regarded as an avatar of Vishnu
    Achintyavirya, of Unimaginable Prowess
    Achyuta, the Unfallen
    Adhoksaja, Born under an Axle
    Chakrayudha, whose Weapon is a Discus
    Govinda, Finder of Cows
    Hari, Tawny
    Hrishikesha: the name may be divided to mean "lord [isha] of the senses [hrishika]" or "with erect [hrishi] hair of the head [kesha]," i.e., "Spike-haired." The latter seems the more likely meaning.
    Janardana, Exciter of Men
    Keshava, Long-haired
    Keshisudana, Subduer of [the anti-god] Keshin
    Madhava, Descendant of Madhu
    Madhusudana, Slayer of [the anti-god] Madhu
    Sharngadhanvan, [the one who bears the] Antelope-horn Bow
    Vasudeva, Son of Vasudeva
    Yadunandana, Joy of the Yadus
Kunti, wife of Pandu, legitimate mother of the five Pandavas and illegitimate mother of Karna
    Pritha, another name of Kunti
Kurus, the cousins and enemies of the Pandavas
Nakula and Sahadeva, twin sons of Pandu and Madri, and of the Ashvins
    Madriputrau, Sons of Madri
    Yamau, the Twins
Narada, a wandering sage
Pandu, father of the five Pandava brothers
Parikshit, "the Remainder," the son of Abhimanyu
Prajapati ("Lord of Creatures"), the Creator
Sanjaya, the bard/charioteer of Dhritarashtra
    Gavalgani, Son of Gavalgana
    Sutaputra, Son of a Bard/Charioteer
Shiva, the Auspicious one
    Mahadeva, the great god
    Rudra, the Roarer
    Trishulin, Trident-bearer
Subhadra, sister of Krishna, wife of Arjuna
Uddhava, a Yadava, friend and counselor of Krishna

Vasudeva, father of Krishna
  Anankadundubhi, [at whose birth] Drums Beat
  Sauri, Son of Suri
Vidura, son of Vichitravirya and a slave girl
  Kshattri, Servant, Son of a Kshatriya father and a Shudra mother
Vishnu, a god
  Hari, Golden, Tawny
  Narayana, Son of the [original] Man
Vrishnis, the people of whom the Pandavas are a part
Vyasa, sage, author of the *Mahabharata* and father of Dhritarashtra, Pandu, and Vidura
  Dvaipayana, of the Island [where he was born]
  Krishna, the Dark One
  Parasharya, son of Parashara
  Satyavatiputra, son of Satyavati
  Yadavi, of the Yadava clan
Yudhishthira, the king who was the first-born son of Pandu, also son of Dharma
  Ajatashatru, Having No [equal] Enemy
  Bharata, Descendant of King Bharata
  Bharatarshabha, Bull of the Bharatas
  Bharatasattama, Best of the Bharatas
  Dharmaja, Son of Dharma
  Dharmatmaja, Son of Dharma
  Dharmaraja, Dharma King
  Dharmasuta, Son of Dharma
  Kaunteya, Son of Kunti
  Kuntiputra, Son of Kunti
  Kururaja, King of the Kurus
  Kurudvaha, Scion of the Kurus
  Kurukulodvaha, Scion of the Kuru Family
  Pandava, Son of Pandu
  Pandavanam dhuramdhara, Bearer of the Yoke of the Pandavas
  Partha, Pritha's Son

Appendix 3: Minor Characters and Classes of Beings

A. Minor Characters

Alayudha, a Rakshasas
All-Gods, a class of gods in heaven
Babhru, a prominent Yadava
  Akrura, not cruel

Bahlika, younger brother of Shantanu
Bhagadatta, a prince of Pragjyotisha
Bhojas, Yadava people associated with Krishna
Bhurishravas, a son of Somadatta king of the Bahlikas; a Kuru
Chekitana, a prince, ally of the Pandavas
Chitrasena, a sage
Dhrishtadyumna, a son of Drupada, brother of Draupadi; killed by Ashvatthaman
Dhrishtaketu, a king of Chedi
Drona, preceptor of both the Pandava and Kaurava princes
Drupada, king of the Panchalas, father of Dhrishtradyumna and Shikhandin
Duhshasana, a son of Dhritarashtra
Dvaraka, the capital of the Vrishnis, on the shore of the Arabian Sea
Gada, Krishna's younger brother
Gandiva, name of Arjuna's bow
Ghatotkacha, son of Bhima and a female Rakshasi
Hardikya, a Bhoja king, the son of Hridika, also called Kritavarman
Jalasandha, a prince
Kripa, also called Gautama, son of the sage Sharadvat; the Brahmin whom Bhishma had appointed the teacher of the sons of Pandu and Dhritarashtra; uncle of Ashvatthaman
Kritavarman, a Bhoja king, the son of Hridika, also called Hardikya
Kubera, god of riches and treasure, ruler of the Northern quarter
Madri/Madravati, Pandu's second wife, mother (by the Ashvins) of Nakula and Sahadeva
Mandatri, a king
Panchajanya, Krishna's conch. Krishna took the conch Panchajanya from an anti-god named Panchajana, Ruler of Five Peoples (the five classes of beings—gods, humans, Gandharvas and Apsarases, serpents, and ancestors).
Pradyumna, son of Krishna and Rukmini, also called Rukmininandana, "Joy of Rukmini"
Prishadhra, a king who fought on the side of the Pandavas
Purukutsa, a king, son of Mandhatri
Rudras, a class of storm gods
Rukmini, one of Krishna's wives, mother of Pradyumna
Sahadeva, son of Jarasandha
Sahasrachitya, a king, grandfather of Shatayupa
Samba, son of Krishna and Rukmini
Satrajit, father of Satyabhama
Satyabhama, also called Satvati, daughter of Satrajit, a wife of Krishna
Satyaki, a Vrishni cousin of Krishna. Also called Shaineya, Shini's son, and Yuyudhana, pugnacious
Shailalaya, a king, grandfather of Bhagadatta

Shakuni, the brother of Gandhari, a counselor of Duryodhana; a sharp dice-player
Shala, a son of Dhritarashtra
Shalya, a king of Madra, brother of Madri
Shantanu, a king, father of Bhishma and of Vichitravirya
Shashaloman, a king
Shatayupa, a royal sage
Shikhandin, the reincarnation of Amba, born as Shikhandini
Soma, the plant of immortality; also the drink of immortality, and the moon (where the ambrosial drink is stored)
Somadatta, a king
Sushena, son of Karna
Tumburu, a sage
Vasavas, wind gods
Vasu, one of eight gods who were cursed to become born as humans; Bhishma is the last of them
Virata, a king
Vishvavasu, a sage
Vrishaka, a king, son of Subala
Vrishasena, son of Karna
Yadava, a descendant of Yadu; the Yadavas are Krishna's clan, while the Bharatas and Kauravas are descended from Puru
Yama, god of the dead. Also called Vaivasvata, son of Vivasvan (the sun)
Yuyudhana, pugnacious, a name of Satyaki
Yuyutsu, Dhritarashtra's only surviving son

B. Classes of Beings

Andhakas, a group of people related to Krishna
Apsaras, a heavenly water nymph
Asura, a celestial anti-god, enemy of the gods
Charana, a celestial musician
Daitya, an anti-god
Danava, an anti-god, a son of Danu
Deva, a god
Dvapara, the third of the four Yugas or ages
Gandharva, a celestial musician
Guhyaka, a goblin
Kimkara, a servant or a type of ogre
Pishacha, a flesh-eating ogre
Punyajana, a class of celestial beings
Rakshasa, an earth-bound anti-god

Sadhyas, a class of gods who live in heaven, "To Be Propitiated"
Siddhas, "perfected beings," heavenly creatures
Suta caste, Charioteers, a kind of chauffeur, bodyguard, and private secretary combined
Yatudhana, a kind of goblin

Appendix 4: The Earlier Lives of the Protagonists of the Last Books of the *Mahabharata*

Book One. The Beginning. King Janamejaya asked the bard Vaisampayana, the pupil of the sage Vyasa, to tell him the story that Vyasa had composed about Janamejaya's ancestors. Janamejaya was the son of Parikshit and the great-grandson of Arjuna; Vyasa was Arjuna's grandfather. Vaisampayana began at the beginning, when, in order to relieve the burden of the Earth by killing off the over-numerous kings in battle, the gods and anti-gods became incarnate on earth as human kings. Then:

Vyasa's mother, Satyavati, married king Santanu. Santanu's son Bhishma (by a previous liaison with the river Ganges) agreed to remain celibate so that Satyavati's sons would be Santanu's heirs. But those sons died childless, and Vyasa returned to father three sons on the widowed queens: those sons were Pandu, Dhritarashtra, and Vidura. Pandu became the king.

Pandu married Kunti and Madri, but as he was cursed to be unable to beget sons, five gods fathered the official sons of Pandu, called the Pandavas: Kunti gave birth to Yudhishthira, son of Dharma; Bhima, son of Vayu, the wind; and Arjuna, son of Indra, king of the gods. (Kunti had previously, and secretly, given birth to Karna, son of the Sun god, but had abandoned him, so that Karna was raised as the son of low-caste charioteers and bards, Sutas). Madri gave birth to the twins Sahadeva and Nahula, sons of the twin gods called the Ashvins. Dhritarashtra, who was born blind, married Gandhari and begat a hundred sons upon her, known as the Kauravas, "the descendants of Kuru," incarnations of various anti-gods. The eldest was Duryodhana.

Pandu died, and Dhritarashtra reigned during Yudhishthira's minority.

In Hastinapur, the cousins, sons of Pandu and Dhritarashtra, were educated together by the Brahmins Kripa and Drona, who also educated their other cousins the Vrishnis, the best of whom was Krishna (the son of Kunti's brother Vasudeva). Drona had grown up with Drupada, ruler of the neighboring kingdom of Panchala; he came to Hastinapur with his son, Ashvatthaman, but Arjuna was his greatest pupil, the one to whom Drona gave magic weapons. The Pandavas rejected Karna because of his apparent low birth, but Duryodhana accepted him as a valuable ally. Drupada had a son, Dhrishtadyumna, who became another pupil of Drona, and a daughter, Draupadi, who eventually married all five of the Pandavas. Dhritarashtra gave the Pandavas half the kingdom, known as the Khandava territory, and they made their capital at Indraprastha. Arjuna carried off Krishna's sister Subhadra and married her, and they had a son, Abhimanyu. Draupadi bore a son to each of the five Pandavas.

The fire god summoned Arjuna and Krishna to help him destroy the Khandava forest and all the creatures in it, which they did, thus also clearing a space for their kingdom. In gratitude, Fire gave Arjuna magic weapons.

Book Two: The Assembly Hall. During Yudhishthira's royal consecration, Duryodhana persuaded Yudhishthira to engage in a game of dice against Shakuni, Duryodhana's maternal uncle, a notorious dice-player. Through trickery, Shakuni won from Yudhishthira his entire kingdom, and all five brothers, and Draupadi. Duryodhana's brother Duhshasana was sent to bring Draupadi into the great assembly hall; he dragged her in by her hair, though she was wearing only a cloth stained by her menstrual blood, and Duryodhana mocked her by exposing his thigh to her. Bhima vowed to drink Duhshasana's blood and to break Duryodhana's thigh. Dhritarashtra ruled that the brothers and Draupadi could go free, but when Yudhishthira lost yet another throw of the dice, they had to go into exile for thirteen years, twelve in the forest and one in disguise in a neighboring kingdom.

Book Three: The Forest. Near the end of the Pandavas' long forest exile, the god Dharma appeared in the Dvaita forest in disguise to test Yudhishthira, who passed the test.

Book Four: King Virata. The Pandavas and Draupadi spent a year in disguise in the court of King Virata. At the end of the year, Arjuna married Virata's daughter Uttama, and eventually they had a son, Parikshit.

Book Five: Preparations. When Duryodhana refused to restore their kingdom to the Pandavas, the two sides prepared for battle on the Field of the Kurus. Krishna and Dhrishtadyumna allied themselves with the Pandavas, and Bhishma (as commander) and Krishna's friend Kritavarman with the Kauravas.

Book Six: Bhishma. Before the first great battle, Arjuna hesitated to kill his kinsmen and teachers. Krishna, who was acting as Arjuna's charioteers, persuaded him to fight, in a discourse known as the *Bhagavad Gita*.

Book Seven: Drona. Arjuna's young son Abhimanyu was killed when he was alone against many armed men, having lost the protection that had been promised to him. As Drona was fighting on the Kaurava side and causing great carnage among the Pandava warriors, Bhima killed an elephant named Ashvatthaman, which was also the name of Drona's son. Krishna urged Yudhishthira to lie to Drona, and Yudhishthira said to Drona, "Ashvatthaman is dead" (adding, under his breath, "the elephant"). Drona, no longer wanting to live, laid aside his weapons and entered a yogic trance, and Dhrishtadyumna cut off his head.

Book Eight: Karna. Bhima killed Duhshasana and drank his blood, in fulfillment of his vow. When Karna's chariot was stuck in the mud, Arjuna violated the warrior's code by beheading Karna before he could remount his chariot.

Book Nine: Shalya. After Sahadeva killed Shakuni, Duryodhana was the only one of Dhritarashtra's sons still alive. Bhima, in violation of the rules of war, broke Duryodhana's thighs with his club. The Pandava armies took over the deserted Kaurava camp, which was full of the spoils of war, but the five Pandavas and Satyaki decided to spend the night outside and to camp on the river.

Book Ten: The Massacre at Night. Ashvatthaman, Kripa, and Kritavarman took refuge in a forest and then went back to the camp where the Pandava armies were asleep. They killed Dhrishtadyumna and Draupadi's five sons and all the Panchalas, and then they set fire to the camp. Only Dhrishtadyumna's charioteers escaped, to bring the news of the slaughter to Duryodhana, who then died. Yudhishthira learned that his army had been destroyed. Draupadi began a fast to death, which she vowed to abandon only when Ashvatthaman would be killed. Ashvatthaman released a magic weapon to destroy all the Pandavas; Arjuna in turn released an equally powerful counter weapon; together they were capable of destroying the world. Vyasa, who was there with Ashvatthaman, persuaded Arjuna to withdraw his weapon, but Ashvatthaman was able only to divert his weapon to the wombs of all the Pandava women, making them barren. Krishna promised to revive the fetus that Abhimanyu's widow Uttara was carrying in her womb; eventually she gave birth to Parikshit. Ashvatthaman was condemned to wander the earth in misery for three thousand years. He gave the Pandavas the jewel that he always wore on his head, and they brought it back to Draupadi. She gave up her fast and gave the jewel to Yudhishthira.

Book Eleven: The Women. Vidura and Vyasa consoled Dhritarashtra and set out with Gandhari and the Kuru women to perform the rites for the dead on the field of battle. Krishna and the Pandavas came to meet them. The women on both sides mourned the dead. Gandhari cursed Krishna for having failed to prevent the slaughter and predicted his death and the end of the Vrishnis. Krishna blamed her for not stopping her son Duryodhana. They performed the rites for the dead.

Book Twelve: The Peace. Bhishma, lying on a bed of arrows, discoursed at great length on the nature of kingship and dharma to Yudhishthira, who wanted to renounce his kingdom.

Book Thirteen: The Teaching. Bhishma continued to talk about dharma and finally died.

Book Fourteen: The Horse Sacrifice. The Pandavas reconquered their kingdom. Uttara gave birth to Parikshit, stillborn, but Krishna revived him. Yudhishthira performed a horse sacrifice to atone for the Pandavas' destruction of their Kaurava cousins.

Book Fifteen. Living in the Ashram. The Pandavas, with Dhritarashtra and Vidura, ruled the kingdom. After fifteen years, Dhritarashtra and Gandhari, with Kunti, Vidura, and Sanjaya, retired to the forest to engage in *tapas*. The Pandavas came to visit them. Vidura used his yogic powers to abandon his body and enter Yudhishthira's body. To console Dhritarashtra, Vyasa conjured up a vision of the dead warriors on both sides, now reconciled. The Pandavas returned to Hastinapur. Dhritarashtra, Gandhari, and Kunti died in a forest fire. The Pandavas performed their funeral rites.

Book Sixteen: The Battle of the Clubs. Thirty-six years after the battle, the Pandavas learned that Gandhari's curse had come true, and that Krishna's Yadava people (the Vrishnis, Andhakas, and Bhojas) had died in a drunken quarrel, killing one another with clubs magically transformed from blades of grass. Satyaki and Kritavarman had died, as had several of Krishna's sons, inciting Krishna to annihilate them all. Only Krishna and Balarama survived. The ocean flooded the city of Dvaraka. Balarama died, and Krishna, shot by a hunter, ascended to heaven. Arjuna performed their funeral rites.

Book Seventeen: The Great Departure. Yudhishthira installed Parikshit, his nephew, as king in Hastinapur, under the preceptorship of Kripa. The five Pandavas and Draupadi renounced the world, circumambulating the earth. When they came to Mount Meru, they began to climb, but one by one they fell, leaving only Yudhishthira and a dog that had been following him. Indra appeared in a chariot, inviting Yudhishthira to enter heaven, but when Indra insisted that dogs were not allowed in heaven, and Yudhishthira refused to abandon the dog, the dog revealed his true form as Dharma and praised Yudhishthira for his devotion to his devotee. Yudhishthira entered heaven and asked to go where his brothers and Draupadi were.

Book Eighteen: Climbing to Heaven. The first person Yudhishthira saw in heaven was Duryodhana, seated in splendor. Furious, Yudhishthira refused to remain in heaven with Duryodhana and without his brothers and Draupadi. At his request, the messenger of the gods took him down to a foul and excruciating hell. There he found his brothers, including Karna, and Draupadi; they begged him to remain there, as the cool breeze from his body erased their torment. Yudhishthira vowed to remain there. Indra and the gods appeared and explained that Yudhishthira had experienced merely a deceptive illusion of hell, in punishment for his deception of Drona. His brothers were all in heaven. Yudhishthira bathed in the Ganges and took on a heavenly body. Then he found all the Pandavas and Kauravas in heaven, devoid of their mutual enmity, as he had to relinquish his enmity with Duryodhana. They were all united with the gods of whom they had been the earthly incarnations.

Appendix 5: Bibliography for Further Reading

1. The *Mahabharata* in Sanskrit

Mahabharata, for the first time critically edited by Vishnu S. Sukthankar, S. K. Belvalkar, et al. Poona: Bhandarkar Oriental Research Institute, 1933–1969.
Mahabharata, with the commentary of Nilakantha. Bombay: Jagadishvara, 1862.

2. A Selection of Translations of the Entire Mahabharata into English, in Chronological Order

K. M. Ganguli, ed. P. C. Roy. *The Mahabharata of Krishna-Dwaipayan. Translated into English Prose.* 12 vols. Calcutta: Bharat Press, 1883–96.
M. N. Dutt. *A Prose English Translation of the Mahabharata. Translated Literally from the Original Sanskrit Text.* 2 vols. Calcutta: Oriental Publishing, 1962. (First published 1895–1905 by H. C. Dass, Calcutta: Elysium Press).
John D. Smith. *The Mahabharata: An Abridged Translation.* London: Penguin Books, 2009.
Bibek Debroy. *The Mahabharata.* 10 vols. Haryana, India: Penguin, 2015.

3. A Selection of Translations of Individual Books of the Mahabharata, in Order of the Books Translated

Books 1–5. J. A. B. van Buitenen. *The Mahabharata.* Book 1, *The Book of the Beginning.* 1973. Books 2–3, *The Book of the Assembly Hall; The Book of the Forest,* 1975; Books 4–5, *The Book of Virata; The Book of the Effort,* 1978. Chicago: University of Chicago Press.
Book 2. Paul Wilmot. *Book 2, The Great Hall.* Clay Sanskrit Library. New York: New York University Press, JJC Foundation, 2005.
Book 3. W. J. Johnson. *Book 3, The Forest.* Clay Sanskrit Library. New York: New York University Press, JJC Foundation, 2005.
Books 4–5. Kathleen Garbutt. *Book 4: Virata. Book 5: Preparations for War.* Clay Sanskrit Library 2006, 2009.
Book 6. Alex Cherniak. *Book 6: Bhishma.* Clay Sanskrit Library, 2009.
Book 7. Vaughn Pilikian. *Book 7 Drona.* Clay Sanskrit Library, 2009.
Book 8. Adam Bowles. *Book 8. Karna.* Clay Sanskrit Library, 2009.
Book 9. Justin Meiland. *Book 9. Shalya.* Clay Sanskrit Library, 2009.
Book 10. W. J. Johnson. *The Sauptikaparvan of the Mahabharata. The Massacre at Night. A New Verse Translation.* New York: Oxford University Press, 1998.
—Kate Crosby. Book 10. *Dead of Night.* Clay Sanskrit Library. 2009.
Book 11. James L. Fitzgerald. *The Mahabharata 11. The Book of the Women.* Chicago: University of Chicago Press, 2004.
—Kate Crosby. Book 11. *The Women.* Clay Sanskrit Library. 2009.
Book 12. Fitzgerald, James L. *The Mahabharata 12. The Book of Peace, Part One.* Chicago: University of Chicago Press, 2004.
Book 12, Vol. 3. Alexander Wynne. *Peace: The Book of Liberation.* Clay Sanskrit Library, 2009.

4. Some Contemporary Retellings of the *Mahabharata*, Alphabetically by Author

Carriere, Jean-Claude. *The Mahabharata: A Play Based Upon the Indian Classical Epic*. Trans. Peter Brook. London: Methuen, 1987. The basis of Peter Brook's film *The Mahabharata* (Connoisseur Video, 1989).

Divakaruni, Chitra Banerjee. *The Palace of Illusions*. New York: Random House, 2008.

Nair, Karthika. *Until the Lions: Echoes from the Mahabharata*. Delhi: HarperCollins India, 2015.

Patil, Amruta. [Book 1] *Adi Parva: Churning of the Ocean*. Noida: HarperCollins India, 2012.

Patil, Amruta. [Book 10] *Sauptik: Blood and Flowers*. Noida: HarperCollins Publishers India, 2016.

Pattanaik, Devdutt. *Jaya: An Illustrated Retelling of the Mahabharata*. Delhi: Penguin Books, 2010.

Ray, Pratibha. *Yajnaseni: The Story of Draupadi*. Trans. Pradip Bhattacharya. Delhi: Rupa, 2002.

Tharoor, Shashi. *The Great Indian Novel*. New York: Penguin, 1989.

5. Some Books about the *Mahabharata*, Alphabetically by Author

Bose, Buddhadev. *The Book of Yudhisthir: A Study of the Mahabharata of Vyas*. Trans. Sujit Mukherjee. Hyderabad: Sangam Books, 1986.

Bowles, Adam. *Dharma, Disorder and the Political in Ancient India: The Apaddharmaparvan of the Mahabharata*. Leiden: Brill, 2007.

Brockington, John. *The Sanskrit Epics*. Leiden: Brill, 2008.

Brodbeck, Simon, and Brian Black, eds. *Gender and Narrative in the Mahabharata*. London: Routledge, 2007.

Dandekar, R. N., ed. *The Mahabharata Revisited*. Delhi: Sahitya Akademi, 1990.

Earl, James W. *Beginning the Mahabharata: A Reader's Guide to the Frame Stories*. Woodland Hills, CA: South Asian Studies Association, 2011.

Goldman, Robert P. *Gods, Priests, and Warriors: The Bhrgus of the Mahabharata*. New York: Columbia University Press, 2015.

Gonzalez-Reimann, Luis. *The Mahabharata and the Yugas: India's Great Epic Poem and the Hindu System of World Ages*. New York: Peter Lang, 2002.

Hawley, Nell Shapiro, and Sohini Sarah Pillai. *Many Mahabharatas*. Albany: State University of New York Press, 2021.

Hiltebeitel, Alf. *Rethinking the Mahabharata. A Reader's Guide to the Education of the Dharma King*. Chicago: University of Chicago Press, 2001.
Hiltebeitel, Alf. *The Ritual of Battle: Krishna in the Mahabharata*. Ithaca, NY: Cornell University Press, 1976.
Hudson, Emily T. *Disorienting Dharma: Ethics and the Aesthetics of Suffering in the Mahabharata*. Oxford: Oxford University Press, 2013.
Karve, Iravati K. *Yuganta: The End of an Epoch*. Poona: Deshmukh Prakashan, 1969.
Katz, Ruth C. *Arjuna in the Mahabharata: Where Krishna Is, There Is Victory*. Columbia: University of South Carolina Press, 1989.
Mitra, Ananda. *Television and Popular Culture in India: A Study of the Mahabharat*. Delhi: Sage, 1993.
Shalom, Naama. *Re-ending the Mahabharata: The Rejection of Dharma in the Sanskrit Epic*. Albany: State University of New York Press, 2017.
Sharma, Arvind, ed. *Essays on the Mahabharata*. Leiden: E. J. Brill, 1991; Delhi: Motilal Banarsidass, 2007.
Shastri, Ajay Mitra, ed. *Mahabharata: The End of an Era (Yuganta)*. Shimla: India Institute of Advanced Study, 2004.
Subramanian, M. V. *The Mahabharata Story: Vyasa and Variations*. Madras: Higginbothams (Private), 1967.
Varadpande, M. L. *Mahabharata in Performance*. Delhi: Clarion Books, 1990.

Appendix 6: Technical Textual Notes

15.26.18a reading *tadā* for *tava*, with D5.
15.26.21-22 This verse is in *triṣṭubh*.
15.28.7a reading *ākumārāś*, with D5, S (except G2).
15.28.16+ K3 adds the italicized *triṣṭubh*.
15.30.10c reading *śīghrajavanau* with Dn, D1, 2.
15.32.5 This verse and all verses up to 15.32.18, at the end, are in *triṣṭubh*.
15.33.36 This verse has three lines.
15.36.6. D4-6, 8, S add the two italicized *shlokas*.
15.36.13b Where I have Subhadra, the text here actually reads Satvati, which is a name of Satyabhama, one of Krishna's wives. But since Satyabhama plays no part in this part of the story, and Subhadra is mentioned several times as being present here, and since Subhadra's name appears in precisely the same relationship to Kunti and Draupadi at 15.37.2, I think the poet mixed up his women here, and I've substituted Subhadra for Satvati. There are many alternative readings for other parts of this verse, though not for Satvati/Satyabhama.
15.36.15 This verse has three lines.

APPENDICES 179

15.36.24d reading *tapodhanaiḥ* for *tapodhanāḥ*, with K, G5, M2-5.
15.36.33f This verse has three lines, and I read *pitar* for *pitaḥ*, with T2, M2, and G1. Though the reading of *pitaḥ* is also possible, since Vyasa is after all Dhritarashtra's father, nowhere else does Dhritarashtra address Vyasa as his father.
15.37.12 This verse has three lines.
15.38.3b reading *tvāgamais,* with D9.
15.38.8 This verse has three lines.
15.39.11 This verse has three lines.
15.39.12 This verse has three lines.
15.41.16b reading *yān avāpya raṇe hatāḥ,* with K4.
15.41.17 This verse has three lines.
15.41.25 reading *deśa* for *deha,* with K2, 2.5, B1, 2, 3-5, Dn, D1, 2, 5, 7, 9, G1, 2, M.
15.41.25+ D4-5, 8; S. I added the italicized *shloka*.
15.41.28 This verse has three lines.
15.44.8b reading *diṣṭe na,* i.e., inserting a space between *diṣṭe* and *na*, without manuscript support. (John Smith does this, too.) With apologies to Alcoholics Anonymous.
15.44.34 This verse has three lines.
15.44.39c reading *maivam* with D4.
15.44.48 This verse has three lines.
15.45.21 This verse has three lines.
15.45.41 This verse has three lines.
15.46.12 This verse has three lines.
15.46.20+ G1, 5, M 3-4 add the final two italicized *shlokas*.
16.2.12 This verse has only one line.
16.2.15+ K B1-5 Dm D1-4,5 (marg.), 7-9, T3 add the italicized half *shloka*.
16.2.17+ M4 adds the italicized half *shloka*.
16.3.2 There is much variation on this verse in K4, K3, 5, N (except D6), T2, 3.
16.3.4+ This verse has three lines. N (except D5. 6), T3 add the italicized half *shloka*.
16.3.13+ T1 inserts the italicized half *shloka*.
16.3.17a K1-3, 5, B2, T2, 3, G1-3, 5, M, and Js have "thirteenth" in place of "fourteenth," a reading that tries to make a somewhat different sense of this complicated system.
16.3.20+ K3 inserts the italicized *shloka*.
16.4.1+ N (except D4) T2, 3 add the first italicized *shloka*, and K3, 5 continues and adds the next *shloka* and a half.
16.4.4+ Verses 16.4.4 and .5 are in *triṣṭubh*. After verse 5, D5, 6, T2, 4, and G1, 2 insert the italicized *shloka*.
16.4.11b reading *kṛtāñjaliḥ* instead of *kṛtāñjaliṃ*, with K2, 4, B2, D2, 5, T1, 2, 4, G2, 3, 5, M1-2.

16.4.25a reading *gaccheddhi* for *gacchāmi*, with T2. Stretching the verb to include a causative meaning would yield, "I will make him go on the path ..." but this seems unjustified.
16.4.39a B5, Dn, D2-4, 9, T3 read *āvidhyānvidhya*, "piercing even what could not be pierced."
16.4.42a reading *tad* rather than *taṃ*, with most of the variants.
16.5. All twenty-five verses of this chapter are in *triṣṭubh*, some of them (16.5.5, -7, -15, -20) with six lines.
16.5.5 This verse has six lines.
16.5.6 This verse has six lines.
16.5.12 This is a problematic verse, with many variants, none quite satisfactory, but the general sense is clear enough. Several manuscripts have *mahārṇavaṃ* in the last line, and that's a better reading to begin with. Some have *yaḥ sa* for *yena* in that line.
16.5.15 This verse has six lines.
16.5.17b reading *uktaṃ hi* for *uktaḥ sa*, with K1, 4, B2, 4, D3, 7, T3, G 3.
16.5.18+ Dn, D2, 5, 6, 9, T, G1-3, 5, M add the italicized *triṣṭubh*.
16.5.21+ D5, 6, T2, 4, G1, 2 add the italicized *triṣṭubh*.
16.5.25+ T G1-3, 4, M, D5, 6 add five italicized *triṣṭubhs*, which the critical edition designates as Appendix I, No. 1.
16.6.8d Dn, D2, 4, 7-9 have pools, *hradāṃ*, for *grahāṃ*, crocodiles; K4 and D1 have trees, *drumāṃ*.
16.6.13a reading *Satyabhāmā* for *tataḥ satyā*, with K1, 2, 5, D5, 6, T1, 3, 4, G1-3, 5, and M.
16.7.2+ N (except D5, 6, K3) add the italicized *shloka*.
16.7.3b This verse has three lines. The sons are mentioned twice; T4 reads "fathers" instead of the first "sons," but this makes little sense.
16.7.11+ K, B1-6, D (except D5, 6), T2, 3 add the four and a half-italicized *shlokas*.
16.7.14 This verse has three lines.
16.8.30a reading *caiṣāṃ* for *caiva*, with K3, T3, G5, M 2, 4, 5.
16.8.32 This verse has three lines.
16.8.34 This verse has three lines.
16.8.40+ K, B1-5, D (except D6) add the first italicized *shloka* and K3, 5 add three and a half *shlokas*.
16.8.46+ M4 adds the first italicized *shloka* and M1 adds the second *shloka*.
16.8.52+ B2, 3 adds the italicized half-*shloka*.
16.8.53+ M1 adds the italicized one and a half *shlokas*.
16.8.72+ K3, 5, Dn2, D9 add the italicized shloka.
16.9.4+ K3, 5, Dn, D2-5, 8, 9, T3, G1 add the italicized line.
16.9.6+ M4 adds the italicized shloka.
16.9.7+ D5, 6, T2, 4, G1, 2, M1 add the two italicized *shlokas*.

16.9.12a The critical edition chooses the palatal s, *mṛśyāmi*, "I cannot grasp it." But reading, with D7, the dental s, *mṛsyāmi*, gives a better sense: "I cannot bear it."

16.9.18+ K3, 5 add the italicized *shloka*.

16.9.25+ D 5, 6, T 2-4, G 1,2 add the italicized *shloka*.

16.9.27+ D5, 6, T 2-4, G1, 2, M1, 4 add the italicized *shloka*.

17.1.3c Nilakantha (with Dn, D2-4, K4) reads *kālapāśa*, "the noose of time," in place of *karmanyāsa*, "renouncing action."

17.1.11a Though there is no manuscript support for it, surely *mātṛbhiḥ* should be *bhrātṛbhiḥ*.

17.1.11+ K2-5, Dn, D2-4, 7, T2, 3 add the one-and-a-half italicized *shlokas*.

17.1.17+ D5, 6, S add the two-and-a-half italicized shlokas.

17.1.25c-d The *sandhi* of *kauravya ulūpī* is irregular in either case, but if we assume that the final "a" of Kauravya is short, it is yet another vocative for Janamejaya. If we assume that it is long, it could be a patronymic for Ulupi. G3 has *kauravyā*, which still leaves us with irregular sandhi but at least justifies giving the epithet to Ulupi, as I have done.

17.1.34d *mā* is a misprint for *māṃ*, as the critical apparatus makes clear.

17.2.1+ K2, 3 add the four italicized *shlokas* after 17.2.1, though I think the inserted passage would have fit better after 17.1.44.

17.2.10+ K3 adds the italicized *shloka*.

17.2.20c The phrase with *kasya* recurs at 18.3.46 in the same context, asking how it is that a good person ended up in a bad place, but there it makes different sense because it is asking about one out of a group. Here it might mean, "What then made him undergo a bad change . . .?" Or we might read *kaścid* (with K2 and G3) for *kasya*: "Did he then undergo some bad change...?"

17.3.8 From here through verse 17.3.16 the meter is *upajāti*.

17.3.11+ N (except D6) T3 add the four italicized lines in *upajāti*.

17.3.14 The last line has an extra syllable.

17.3.28c reading *bhrātṛnapaśyan*, "not seeing his brothers," with K3, D5, S, in place of *devānāmantrya*, "saying farewell to the gods."

17.3.36 Nilakantha and K2, 4, 5, B2,4, Dn, D1-4 have *gatā* for *yatra*, still ambiguous.

18.1.11c reading *nivāse* for *nivāso*, with K5, Dn, D2, 3, 9 as well as with Nilakantha.

18.2.18a reading *daṃśamatkuṇayūkābir*, with K3, D3.

18.2.27c reading *kasya* for *kaśca*, with D9. G4 is also a good reading.

18.2.28 reading *mama* for *tava* with D1.

18.3.5. This verse has three lines.

18.3.10+. This verse has three lines. After this verse, D5, 6, T2, 4, G 1, 2, 4 and M1, 2 insert the italicized half *shloka*.

18.3.12+ This verse has three lines. B2, 3 insert the italicized half *shloka*.
18.3.26d reading *śamiṣyasi* for *gamiṣyasi* with K2.
18.3.41+ N (except E5, 6), T3 insert the italicized shloka.
18.4.3 This verse has three lines.
18.4.5d reading *divyena* for *tenaiva*, with K1, 2. If we accept *tenaiva*, the verse seems to mean (as in 18.4.2), "with the very same body," presumably the body that he had on earth; that is, he looked just like that, though he cannot literally have the same body.
18.4.7+ K1 adds the italicized *shloka*.
18.4.13 This verse has three lines.
18.4.14 This verse has three lines.
18.4.16c reading *saha* for *sadā*, with K3, B5, D5, 6, T 1, 2, 4, G1-2, M2-4.
18.5.5 This verse has three lines.
18.5.15d reading *gaṇam āviviśur nṛpa*, with D5, 6, T1, 2, 4, G, and M.
18.5.19 This verse has three lines.
18.5.20+ There are a number of additional italicized passages here. K3; then B, Dn, D2, 3, 4, 7, T3, G1; and then M1, 3 add one line, then two lines, and then two lines, respectively.
18.5.21+ This verse has three lines. N (except D5, 6), T3 add the italicized half *shloka*.
18.5.34+ D 5, 6, T, G, M 1-5 add the italicized *shloka*.
18.5.35+ Dn, D5, 6, S add the italicized *shloka*.
18.5.36+ K2 adds the one-and-a-half italicized *shlokas*.
18.5.37+ K3-5, B, Dn, D1-4, 7-9, T3 and the Bombay edition add two italicized *shlokas*. And then the Bombay edition adds two *shlokas*, D5, 6, 9, T1-4, G, M, add a shloka, then three *shlokas* from D9, and then a *shloka* from the Bombay edition.
18.5.38+ D5, 6, T, G2, 3, 5, M add a *shloka*; T1 adds another half *shloka*, and then two more *shlokas*.
18.5.39+ D5, 6, T1, 2, 4, G, M add the italicized *shloka*, then D5, T1, G3 add two *shlokas*, then T1 adds one and a half *shlokas*.
18.5.41+ K3-5, B, Dn, D1-3, T2-3 add the two italicized *shlokas*.
18.5.44+ D5, 6, T1, 2, 4, G, M add (after 43, but placed here after 44) two-and-a-half italicized *shlokas*, and then G4 alone continues with a *shloka*.
18.5.50 This verse is in *triṣṭubh*.